"Amoda Maa is a fresh, clear voice of the grounded feminine who spe~~~~~~~tly to the heart of anyone hungering for lasting peace i~ ~~~~~~~~~~~~~~in world. The clarity of her realization shines fort~~~~~~~~~~~~~~~~~~or us all to consciously embody the living truth in~~~~~

—**Shanti Einolander**, founder of *ONE Th*

"*Embodied Enlightenment* eloquently challenges us to honestly and intimately meet our experience just as it is, and to awaken out of the trance of the perpetually seeking separate self. This is a deeply illuminating description of how an awakened life transmutes the ordinary arenas of relationships, work, sex, money, the body, and life purpose. A beautifully written, inspiring, and distinctly feminine call to consciously embody the unfolding edge of evolution. I highly recommend it!"

—**John J. Prendergast, PhD**, author of *In Touch*, adjunct professor of psychology at California Institute of Integral Studies, and psychotherapist

"Amoda Maa reminds us that enlightenment is not simply a transcendent spiritual orgasm into knowing ourselves as unchanging awareness; it invites us ever more deeply into our humanity, into the paradoxes of life, with an unconditional embrace. Her voice is a breath of fresh air in its precision and breadth, as well as its depth and down-to-earth parlance. I am sure *Embodied Enlightenment* will become a true companion to those willing to walk an integrated spiritual path."

—**Miranda Macpherson**, author of *Boundless Love*

"With diamond-like clarity, a cup of compassion, and an almost poetic intensity, Amoda Maa debunks the myth of enlightenment, addressing many commonly held concerns and questions about the process of awakening. No topic is off limits in this conversation as she dismantles the scaffolding of our defenses, our beliefs—the very mechanism of seeking itself. I highly recommend this beautifully written and insightful book to anyone at any stage in their spiritual evolution. You are invited to dive in, face your personal wounds with 'courage and tender honesty,' challenge your assumptions, and root the full flowering of your consciousness in the very belly of your humanity."

—**Kirtana**, singer, songwriter, and recording artist of songs for awakening

"Amoda Maa is a gracious and powerful guide who steers a clear and honest path through the mist of confusion and misunderstanding about the awakened state to hold a new, revelatory light to all that was previously unclear or speculated on. Here, the old, outmoded ways of viewing liberation are cast aside for a more informed, enriching vision of enlightenment—one that embraces our twenty-first-century sensibilities and shies away from nothing."

—**Stephen Gawtry**, managing editor of *Watkins Mind Body Spirit Magazine*

"As the invitation to awaken from the dream of separation is being felt more strongly, both on a collective and individual level, so too arises the need for skillful guides familiar with this paradoxical new landscape. Amoda Maa is one such friend on the path; a gentle but rigorous companion on the journey of unfolding to being both fully awake and fully human. *Embodied Enlightenment* is a beautiful and precious gift to an emerging new humanity."

—**Julian Noyce**, founder of Non-Duality Press

"Enlightenment has long been associated with an austere, recluse lifestyle. But today, people fully engaged in worldly responsibilities are waking up. Ancient traditions may not adequately support their awakening in the midst of 'real-world' concerns such as health, finances, relationships, et cetera. Amoda Maa is one of the brightest of a new generation of spiritual teachers who are meeting that need. She has been prepared for this role in a crucible of personal transformation, and is now fulfilling it admirably."

—**Rick Archer**, creator and host of *Buddha at the Gas Pump*

Embodied Enlightenment

LIVING YOUR AWAKENING

IN EVERY MOMENT

AMODA MAA

REVEAL PRESS

AN IMPRINT OF NEW HARBINGER PUBLICATIONS

Publisher's Note

This publication is designed to provide accurate and authoritative information in regard to the subject matter covered. It is sold with the understanding that the publisher is not engaged in rendering psychological, financial, legal, or other professional services. If expert assistance or counseling is needed, the services of a competent professional should be sought.

Distributed in Canada by Raincoast Books

Copyright © 2017 by Amoda Maa Jeevan
        Reveal Press
        An imprint of New Harbinger Publications, Inc.
        5674 Shattuck Avenue
        Oakland, CA 94609
        www.newharbinger.com

Cover design by Amy Shoup

Acquired by Catharine Meyers

Edited by Erin Raber

Cover photos by Rupert Truman

All Rights Reserved

FSC
www.fsc.org
MIX
Paper from
responsible sources
FSC® C011935

Library of Congress Cataloging-in-Publication Data on file

19   18   17

10   9   8   7   6   5   4   3   2   1   First Printing

Contents

Foreword

The teachings and practices of waking up from the suffering of the separate self into the freedom and joy of our true, essential nature date back thousands of years in Asian cultures. Since these teachings were often only available to a select few, and were largely practiced in otherworldly settings such as monasteries and forest hermitages, integrating them with everyday life concerns was never a major focus of Asian spirituality.

What is different today is that these teachings and practices have become widely available to anyone, East or West. As they spread through modern culture, they inevitably bump up against personal concerns, such as psychological health, livelihood, and interpersonal relationships. The challenge then becomes one of seeing and working with these concerns as an integral part of the spiritual journey. And the opportunity this provides is to overcome the age-old split between spiritual and worldly through a secular awakeness that is integrated into everyday life.

One of the biggest obstacles to an integrated spirituality is a phenomenon I dubbed *spiritual bypassing*—the widespread tendency to use spiritual ideas and practices to avoid facing unresolved emotional issues, psychological wounds, and unfinished developmental tasks. This often shows up as a kind of premature transcendence: the attempt to rise above the raw and messy side of our humanness before fully facing and embracing it.

Amoda Maa's book can be seen as a guide to secular awakening as well as an antidote for spiritual bypassing. In a clear and incisive way, she carefully explores the different ways in which spiritual practitioners need to work with their fallible humanness as the pathway for embodying transcendent truth. In her words, "The willingness to embrace personal truth in the search for absolute truth is a necessary component of the authentic embodiment of awakened consciousness." May you dive deep into this book, which is full of genuine, helpful guidance on the journey of waking up, and insight into how this can illumine all the hidden corners of your life.

—John Welwood
Author of *Toward a Psychology of Awakening*

My Story of Awakening

I am often asked about my life and my own story of awakening. For me, the past is very much like a dream and I don't cling to it. So much has changed and continues to change that I cannot find myself in any of it. The only resting place I can find is in consciousness itself, and this is empty of content. As each moment is born and dies, there is nothing here to identify with. However, people want to know something of the human being and not just the spiritual teacher. I know that it helps to hear one another's stories, to make sense of the human experience and touch the universality of what it means to be alive. There are many details and subtleties to my story, but enough is offered here for you to get a taste of what has led me to be where I am and to write this book.

My story has many twists and turns, as do most stories of redemption. The circumstances surrounding my birth were traumatic and shrouded in secrecy and shame, as were my early years. I never knew my real father and my mother and her family covered up the fact that he had left when I was born. Living on a small Greek island in the Mediterranean, where life was still simple and tied to convention, especially with regard to the role of women in the family and society, my mother was burdened with the social and cultural disgrace of being a single parent. Because of this, she created a story about her life that was far from the truth.

When I was born, she was immediately married off to a man from a very different culture than her own and was sent to England to start a new life. The early years were stark and difficult for both my mother and me, but I loved the man I believed to be my father. When he told me, at the age of 13, that he wasn't my father, my whole world fell apart.

During the years that followed, life continued to bring me many unexpected changes that caused me to question who I was and where I came from. Much later, as an adult, this uncertainty about my ancestral roots would form the bedrock of a path of self-inquiry. However, as a young child and adolescent, I experienced these unwelcome events as shocks to my delicate nervous system. Some of these shocks were so dramatic they rendered me mute for periods of time. I was subjected to emotional violence, sexual abuse, abrupt and frequent changes in schooling, the sudden onset of a war on the small island we had moved to, an emergency evacuation by the military back to England, and the loss of our home and all our possessions. This was accompanied by my father's increasing alcoholism, my mother's increasing unhappiness, and their escalating, violent arguments.

For a short while, my mother and I lived in a "home for battered women," until one night she packed our bags and without a word of explanation took us to live with a strange man. I didn't see my father for many years after that. All of these events and more contributed to a deep sense of shame and confusion that would eventually become the catalyst for my spiritual search.

Another thing that became a part of my search for true identity was confusion around communication and language. Communication was always a problem in my home, right from the moment I learned to speak. My mother's native tongue was Greek and it took her several years to acquire a rudimentary command of the English language. My father spoke English very well, but his thick accent and frequent use of German expletives gave away his roots. I, on the other hand, could read and write only English, and I spoke it perfectly. I suppose on some level I must have been bewildered, but this strange set-up was my normality. What wasn't so normal was the strictness of my upbringing. Playing with other children outside of school hours was absolutely forbidden, as was playing with dolls and stuffed toys. Birthdays and Christmas were solemn affairs in which the most exciting gifts, other than pajamas, socks, and school uniforms, were a set of colored pencils and a drawing pad.

The denial of what I believed at the time were basic child-hood rights in the Western world cut right to my core, and I came to the conclusion that I was flawed and deserved to be punished by never getting what I wanted. I felt impure and unworthy, so I prayed to Jesus most nights to cleanse me of my sins, and I prayed to the Holy Mother to take care of me.

As an only child with no friends, I became isolated and introverted, and I retreated into a fantasy world that was my only solace. I spent endless hours creating a secret imaginary life in which every detail was mapped out in incredible intri-cacy, where not only did I have parents who totally adored and understood me, but I also had every single toy and dress I ever wanted, a list of friends who celebrated me, a fascinating life of adventure, and a sense of magic that took me to faraway lands and even into outer space. But this imagined perfect world in which I was perfectly safe, perfectly loved, and perfectly happy never came true.

Eventually, my escape into utopia became a prison. By the time I was a teenager, I had effectively shut myself off from feeling the full vibrancy of life. In fact, I had shut myself off from feeling, period. When I left home at seventeen to go to university, instead of feeling happy and free as I'd expected, I became depressed and socially inadequate. My frequent attempts at suicide led me to believe I'd end up in a mental asylum. I was sent to various psychotherapists and psychiatrists, but none of them could help me. I just sat there looking at the floor, unable to utter a word. It was as if I was separated from both the outer world and my inner world by a thick pane of glass. I could see, but I could not reach out to touch anyone nor reach in to feel anything. I couldn't even talk about this alienation because I denied that there was anything wrong with me.

Surprisingly, in spite of this internal landscape of darkness, I threw myself with great vigor into my academic studies. I stopped believing in Jesus or the Holy Mother as my saviors, and I invested my hope of salvation in the achievement of a Doctorate of Psychology. The seeking mechanism that had fueled my early fantasy world of perfection was still the driving force of my life, only this time it drove me to work incredibly long hours, almost to the exclusion of anything else. I struggled for twelve years against many odds and then over a period of just a few months, unexpectedly and dramatically, the whole edifice of my life collapsed. Not only had I taken some LSD, but I also started long-distance running and meditation. This potent combination allowed a parting of the veils of conditioned perception and revealed the luminous truth of reality. Somehow, in these experiences, I felt as though I was touching the very fabric of existence, and I deeply understood that oneness was my nature, as well as the nature of everything. After this mind-shattering and soul-stirring revelation, the world never looked the same. But it was not an everlasting state, and there was still some unraveling to happen in the three-dimensional world.

At the age of twenty-eight, I found myself homeless and penniless. Not only had my academic career come to an abrupt end, but my long-term boyfriend had left me. My home was repossessed, I became financially bankrupt and without any income, and almost all my material possessions were taken from me. As a result of all these losses in quick succession, I also lost my pride, my confidence, and my dream of a personal utopia. Every single vestige of identity invested in being an academic high-flyer, an urban superwoman, an ideal girlfriend, or any other picture of perfection came tumbling down. It was both devastating and a great relief. Without the usual attachments of modern-day life, and without the burden of trying to "be somebody," I found myself fully open to living in the present. I also found myself naturally drawn to asking the question that had been sown in my early childhood: *Who am I?*

The next seven years were spent in deep inner exploration. A series of mystical and visionary experiences came without warning and were the catalysts for my subsequent immersion in meditation, primal therapy, rebirthing, metaphysics, and a myriad of psycho-spiritual methods. I was particularly drawn to Buddhist and Zen meditation practices and devoted my attention to these. The sanctuary of inner silence seemed very familiar to me. And, unlike my brief encounter with Transcendental Meditation during my university days, which had left me horrified at the intensity of voices in my head, I fell into this space effortlessly. I also loved reading, so I devoured as many traditional and contemporary spiritual books as I could, and along the way I visited various spiritual teachers and enlightened masters. But I quickly discovered that spiritual truth is a fresh discovery, not a learned wisdom. I didn't want to add more handed-down knowledge to my already acquisitive mind. I wanted to find out through my own direct experience. In any case, I wasn't looking for enlightenment, so I stopped chasing a "spiritual high."

What I was really looking for was happiness, and paradoxically it was this search that led me to the land of spirituality— India. While my worldly life was still filled with uncertainty and impoverishment, by this time I did have a roof over my head and was married. But something called me to grow wings and I was willing to leave the relative safety of home and relationship. I arrived at the ashram of the revolutionary mystic Osho, empty-handed and with no prior knowledge about him or his teachings. Although Osho had left his body just a few years earlier, something deep within me immediately stirred and I opened to the unconditional love in his invisible presence. I fell in love with his rebellious spirit, absorbed his words, gave my totality to his unorthodox meditative techniques, and bathed in the silence of solitude for several months. An inner fire that blasted my heart wide open consumed me, and I willingly surrendered to the tantric mystery of existence.

By facing my deep fear of aloneness, I discovered that there was nothing to fear but the idea of fear itself. And by lovingly sitting with this fear, I realized that love is at the core of everything. Somehow this realization allowed me to see that all appearances are impermanent, and this loosened my attachment to the surface reality of form. I stopped searching for a teacher or a teaching; instead, life itself became my guru. For the first time in my life, I felt a certain freedom and joy. Perhaps the many hours spent screaming, shouting, and shaking my way through different forms of psycho-physical therapy and "active meditations" had helped me let go of some of my emotional baggage. Perhaps I had tasted the truth of emptiness. Whatever the reason, I left India feeling reborn and with a new name, Amoda Maa Jeevan, which means "living a joyous life."

Back in England, I started teaching transformational workshops and developed my own unique method of "ecstatic meditation," which included intense breath work, crazy dancing, and wild improvised music. I had stepped out of my introvert's "ivory castle," allowing myself to be seen by the world and growing beyond my limitations. Life was good.

While I was no longer looking for a spiritual high, there was a subtle seeking still going on that had to do with relationship. I still held a deep belief that I needed relationship to give me something I hadn't yet found in myself. I needed another to make me feel complete, and to confirm my worthiness by giving me love in the form of a perfect relationship. I clung to the idea that a soul mate would fulfill all my inner and outer dreams. Unfortunately, the man I'd decided was my soul mate (and my husband) didn't conform to my ideas of a perfect life, and so we raged, battled, and hurt each other, while passionately loving each other, for ten years. One day, seemingly out of the blue, our relationship exploded and there was no mending it. I harnessed enough courage within myself to walk away. Over the next two years, I grieved intensely, attempted to heal my broken heart with all manner of therapies and bodywork, and eventually learned to enjoy my own company and the freedom of living alone.

In the silent space of solitude, a deeper wound revealed itself: the profound existential fear that God had abandoned me. I felt empty and incredibly alone. As I had done many years before, I was sinking into a black hole. Except this time I had enough insight to recognize that this internal darkness was the call to true freedom. I realized that I wanted to be free of the story of "me." I was willing to give up my need for love, relationship, happiness, enlightenment, and even the need for any certainty, but I had no idea how to do this. There was no teacher, no road map, and no instruction manual. Yet I trusted the gentle yet insistent impulse to be still and to stop running away. I chose not to follow the familiar contortions of my mind as I had done a million times before, and instead meet in naked awareness the most primal of fears: annihilation. I opened to not-knowingness and allowed myself to die into this. And in this dying, all notions of self dissolved into emptiness. I suppose I expected a kind of cold nothingness, but instead an incredible joy arose. Without labeling it or packaging it or reinvesting any identity in it, the emptiness revealed a luminosity of being. It had always been here; and, contrary to appearances, I realized I had never been separate from this.

From that moment on I became a lover of what is, unafraid to get right up close and intimate with whatever showed up in my inner and outer world. My suffering became my doorway to freedom. This freedom looks nothing like I had imagined it to be. I'm often asked: "How is your life different after awakening?" I can only say that life goes on as always, it is utterly unchanged, and yet, in meeting everything as it is, everything has changed.

Today, fifteen years later, the waves of phenomenal existence called "my story" continue. Sometimes the sea is stormy, but mostly it is as calm as a millpond. Sometimes there is pain, hardship, and unpleasant feelings, but with much less frequency and ferocity than ever before. Somehow nothing sticks; pain and discomfort don't last very long. I now have an exquisite sensitivity to every nuance of life's movement, and yet nothing interrupts the pristine silence at the core of it all. The radiant jewel that is this silence continues to illuminate the places in my body and mind that are still holding ancient patterns that do not serve the bigger picture of love. It's an ongoing demolition project in which everything that is not true is destroyed. And it becomes subtler as time goes on. Even as I write these words, I cannot possibly say how it will be next year, or next week, or even tomorrow. All I can say is that the filtering of awakeness into my everyday life happens effortlessly, and there's nothing I have to do to make it happen. It is ordinary and it is graceful.

Every person's awakening is unique. The stillness of Ramana Maharshi looks very different compared to the wisdom of Chogyam Trungpa; the secular life of one of today's nonduality teachers looks very different from the monastic life of a Buddhist monk. Inevitably, the outer expression of enlightenment is colored by history, geography, and biography, yet we often look at spiritual teachers, enlightened masters, mystics, and saints and try to model our enlightenment on what we see. We say, "Ah, this is what it looks like!" and the ego tries to make sense of it according to its own predispositions. Ego loves to package "truth" and then claim this package for itself. It's a mistaken belief in a spiritual reward system that keeps us on the wheel of seeking. We often hop around from one teacher or teaching to another, looking for something that conforms to our idea of enlightenment. But truth, like love, is uncontainable. It is untamable, unconditional, and universal.

Perhaps because of my life circumstances, my personality, or my karmic predispositions, that which has revealed itself as the truth of who I really am has also revealed a vision for humanity. This vision is both a revelation of awakened consciousness as it emerges in the fullness of this present moment, and it is a revelation of an awakened world as it is emerging into a future possibility. I do not know exactly what this awakened world will look like, but I do know its fragrance intimately. It is the force of this invisible fragrance that moves me to share this vision with you.

I do not know what this awakening will look like in you. I don't even know if you will awaken or not: it's not for me to say. But I do know that I'm responding to life's impulse by inviting you into a conversation that may trigger this awakening in you. This book is both the invitation and the conversation.

INTRODUCTION

An Invitation to the Most Precious Discovery

There is a momentum pulling us toward an emerging future, and this future holds the potential for a collective awakening that catapults us into the next stage as a species. For the first time in the known story of the cosmos, consciousness is becoming conscious of itself. But consciousness can only become conscious of itself through the vehicle of a living form that has the capacity for self-reflection. This includes being able to reflect on the nature of its own thinking and feeling, its own past and future, its own life and death, and on the nature of awareness itself. As far as we know, human beings are the only life-form on earth with this capacity of self-reflection. Consider then the possibility that a new consciousness and a new humanity is birthing itself through you *as* you. If this is so, could it be that *you* are the single most important factor in this birthing process? Could it be that you are the vehicle through which existence itself is attempting to re-create itself on the next highest level … and that *your* awakening absolutely matters? This book is an invitation to the unfolding of this awakening.

Awakening is the most precious of human experiences. The discovery of this truth is like finding a priceless jewel in the one place where we'd never dream to look: in our own pockets. Once it's found, the trajectory of our lives is irreversibly altered. It is a radical and profound revelation that literally enlightens us by breaking the spell of identification with form to reveal the truth of who we are. This enlightenment means that an ancient burden is lifted and we are finally free to live from the core of our true radiance.

Awakening, or *enlightenment* (these terms are used interchangeably), is traditionally and historically the pinnacle of all spiritual paths. It's also the holy grail of the modern-day spiritual seeker. The journey often starts when we've had enough of the voices in our heads telling us we're not rich enough, not successful enough, not loved enough, or not good enough, and we attempt to find ways to alleviate this type of internal torment. Our investigations may lead us to walk down any number of paths that open the doorway to personal growth. We may invest ourselves in self-help methods, immerse ourselves in ancient and modern meditation practices, or follow a trail of metaphysical philosophies and disciplines. Each one of these promises to provide the key to eternal happiness. While this is a good start, because it gives us a golden glimpse into what is possible beyond our habitual thought patterns, if we continue to be seekers of a spiritual high we never break out of this beautiful prison.

If we're lucky, somewhere along the way we get exhausted by the endless grasping for bliss, and our attention turns inward, to the genuine desire to be free not only of the story of "my suffering," but also of the story of "my happiness." The honest inquiry into both the validity of the story and the validity of the story-maker has the potential to end the journey. It ends when we stop searching for something outside ourselves to save us. It ends when we stop looking for a spiritual practice or a guru or enlightenment or God to give us freedom. In this stopping, we wake up to the reality that we are that which we have been seeking. We are already free.

Whereas awakening is always a surprisingly original experience for the individual, there's nothing essentially new about it from a historic perspective. Individuals have been awakening throughout the ages. Early messengers such as Jesus, Buddha, and Lao Tzu have led the way by pointing to an inner dimension of consciousness. Since then, many enlightened masters have shared the same timeless message in their own unique ways.

This awakened consciousness, although still relatively uncommon, is now flowering within countless ordinary people around the world. Some of these people are becoming the new spiritual teachers; others are expressing this awakened state of being in a very down-to-earth way, through their relationships, their work, and their everyday interactions. And some people are at the leading edge of a new culture that is bringing an enlightened perspective to social, economic, and other global issues.

If you're reading this book, then you, too, are undoubtedly on the journey of awakening. Perhaps you've already tasted the sweet nectar of true liberation and are thirsty for more. And perhaps you want to ask the one question that so many others are asking: "How can I anchor myself within this awakened state when everyday life keeps pulling me back into old ways of thinking?" The very fact that this book is in your hands means that there's a real possibility that discovery of the radiant jewel of your true nature is closer than you think.

The invitation to this momentous opportunity is offered to you right here, amongst these pages. This book does not offer more information to add to your already busy mind. Nor does it offer yet another method or spiritual practice to add to your collection. And it certainly doesn't promise instant enlightenment. Instead, it invites you to consider that something irrevocably new is being birthed from within you in this very moment. This "something new" is the fulfillment of your true life's purpose—and this has enormous ramifications for you not only as an individual, but also for humanity.

Traditional spiritual teachings have all emphasized the cultivation of an inner state of stillness that awakens us to the truth of our being-nature. And they say this is achieved by turning away from worldly activity. While the recognition of our essential nature as this beingness *is* the foundation of awakening, what was relevant thousands of years ago is not so relevant today. An exponential increase of pace and pressure in today's world brings a radically new perspective to enlightenment that asks us to reframe our understanding of what it means to be an awakened human being. What's important now is that awakening is no longer about abandoning or transcending physical reality in order to live a spiritual life; rather, it's about the fulfillment of our divine destiny by living the truth of our inner radiance while in earthly bodies.

What's emerging today is a whole new relationship to life that gives birth to an *authentic* human being. It is a refreshingly contemporary viewpoint that acknowledges the imperative to anchor ourselves within the ground of being while celebrating the emergence of that which we are becoming. Another way of saying this is that it's an embracing of the *absolute* truth of stillness and the *relative* truth of the movement of life. The evolutionary impulse that drives the ever-unfolding nature of existence is calling us to awaken to the pristine perfection of our inner light, and then to fully *embody* and *express* this light amid the imperfection and darkness of the world.

The invitation of this book is for you to collaborate in the birth of something new, for you to take a step toward your divine destiny by being willing to unwaveringly embrace the evolutionary process that wants your awakening to happen … because it is also the awakening of humanity.

PARTICIPATION IN THE AWAKENING PROCESS

Something that has never happened before is happening today: we can *participate* in the awakening process. For historical and cultural reasons, it used to be that enlightenment was an extraordinary experience that happened after many lifetimes of self-purification through seclusion, renunciation, celibacy, and religious vows, which have been the traditional hallmarks of a spiritual life. Mostly this would also demand a guru-disciple relationship, or at least some kind of transmission through a lineage. Today, enlightenment is no longer dependent on external factors, such as spiritual discipline, a monastic life, good karma, or finding the right teacher. However, sometimes a teacher is useful in deepening the awakening process; even reading the words in this book can be a catalyst for that which is already awake in you to more fully reveal itself.

Although awakening itself is the same as it was thousands of years ago, the good news is that it's now more directly available to us in the midst of ordinary life. If you are on any kind of path of self-inquiry, self-healing, or self-help, it's hard to deny the infusion of spiritual awareness into contemporary culture, mostly thanks to the Internet. Although it doesn't always seem so if you read the daily newspapers or watch TV, an increasing number of people are turning their attention to the possibility of awakening in this lifetime.

While awakening is always an act of grace and not something we can "do," there is a frequency field of awakened awareness created by the momentum of individuals who have awakened throughout the ages that makes a transformation of consciousness more available to each of us now. What used to be something mysterious and elusive has now become much more familiar. Spiritual books, videos, teachings, and conversations about enlightenment are now easily accessible. But something more than words and abstractions needs to be in place for this frequency field to penetrate you. Awakening hinges on your *genuine* desire for it. If awakening is to flower in you, you must truly want liberation from everything that is false in you. You must want to give yourself totally to the inquiry into what is true beyond all inherited concepts, ideas, and beliefs.

Perhaps this wanting has already been ignited in you. And maybe this spark has already burst into the flame of desire. When this flame becomes an untamable fire, it flips a switch inside you, and the direction of your destiny is irrevocably altered. It's like turning on the light only to discover that you *are* the light. This in itself is extraordinary. Even though you may have heard words that point to the truth of who you are a thousand times, nothing can prepare you for the naked reality that is revealed when it is experienced. And yet, the living experience of this revelation is also very ordinary. You have simply become consciously aware of the innocent wholeness of your essential nature, which has always been here. It is the you that never was and never will be separate from anything at all. This discovery is the end of suffering and the beginning of freedom—for both you and for the world.

THE PURPOSE OF THIS BOOK

In my role as a spiritual teacher, I meet an incredible variety of people who seek truth. Some of these people have been long-time seekers, some have sat with countless spiritual masters, and others are curious newcomers. They are young, old, and everything in between. They are from all walks of life. I have met yoga teachers, therapists, artists, entrepreneurs, firemen, builders, mothers, fathers, grandparents, and many more. Although I teach primarily in the Western world, I also receive numerous emails from people in other parts of the world, such as Africa and the Middle East. What unites this broad spectrum of people is the burning desire to discover that which is deeper than surface reality. What does it mean to awaken in the midst of ordinary life? Certain questions come to the forefront of the dialogues in my meetings over and over again. Mostly they are questions about the relationship between awakening and the body, love and intimate relationships, money, work, and creativity, as well as questions and concerns about the suffering of the world. It seems that a transcendent experience of enlightenment is not enough these days; people need guidance and support in embodying the light of awakeness in every aspect of their lives, as fully functioning human beings in the modern world with all its complexity.

I wrote this book to address some of these questions and to speak directly to the new paradigm of awakening that is emerging amid challenging times today. What is needed now is not more of the ancient spiritual wisdom passed down through the ages, but a cutting-edge conversation that acknowledges this wisdom as the foundation of awakening and goes beyond that to include a dialogue about topics traditionally excluded from spiritual teachings. Some of these topics and questions include: What's the difference in the way awakeness is expressed in men and women? What happens to sex in awakening? Is there such a thing as an enlightened relationship? Does physical well-being matter in awakening? How do we live selflessly in the modern world? How can money and spirituality be friends? This is uncharted territory. What is coming alive in the minds and hearts of those I meet with is an increasing helplessness in the face of escalating world horrors and a desire for personal empowerment and spiritual awareness. There's an urgency to end the insanity, both within and without, and to find peace in our hearts and on earth at last.

If you, too, are asking these questions, you are undoubt-edly ready to join this new spiritual inquiry. This book is divided into three parts, each with its own offering to the conversation.

Part One: A New Consciousness and a New World shares a vision for humanity that embraces an evolutionary perspective of enlightenment, inviting us to consider that the personal and collective darkness so prevalent today is a catalyst for transfor-mation and liberation. While there's an undeniable need to evolve beyond ego's identification with the world of form, there's also a need to make space for the expression of con-sciousness *through* the ego and the world of form. Can these two seemingly opposed approaches sit side by side?

Many spiritual teachings say that suffering is an illusion and that the world does not exist, but is this really true? Part

One explores the validity of this strictly nondual understanding and asks if it's possible to open to a wider perspective that embraces the totality of the human experience.

Part One also explores the possibility that a new evolutionary frequency is expressing itself through the feminine face of awakening. As an increasing number of women awaken and step into the role of spiritual leadership, what's emerging is a juicier, more fluid, and more holistic expression of the age-old mystery of enlightenment. It seems that awakeness itself is pushing the frontiers of a new conversation that includes the earth-centered wisdom of the sacred feminine. The feminine is more attuned to the subtle physical energies that permeate life and so is concerned with a practical spirituality that includes the messiness of intimate relationships, the body and its well-being, the sustainment of a healthy ecology, how money is used, community, communication, and creative expression. Perhaps this new feminine frequency will allow us to collaborate in the awakening process, in service to ourselves and to humanity. And perhaps it will give us the power to finally take responsibility for whether this world is at war or at peace.

This responsibility starts by stopping the war inside. And this means uprooting all false self-concepts that keep us imprisoned in the illusion of separation, and discovering the luminous truth of that which is unendingly whole and free.

Part Two: Fully Awake and Fully Human explores the journey of inner transformation, busting some of the myths of enlightenment that stand in the way of authentic liberation and illuminating some of the common pitfalls along the way. It investigates important inquiries such as: Does awakening mean the death of ego? What happens to the personality? Does all pain disappear? How does one deal with feelings and emotions?

Is there a meeting place of psychotherapy and spiritual inquiry? Is there a relationship between healing and awakening? Is meditation necessary for awakening?

Part Two also explores what happens beyond awakening, when the recognition of awakeness matures and returns to the world as love, forgiveness, and compassion. And then, how the light of that awakeness emerges into the world to give birth to a new humanity.

Part Three: Living the Truth of Awakening in Everyday Life reveals how the embodiment of awakened consciousness can be anchored in the very fabric of our lives, as it permeates the mind, the heart, and the body, and expresses itself in the world. Here, the conversation becomes more personal, and you, the reader, are invited into an honest personal inquiry, to expose anything that stands in the way of living the truth of awakening in everyday life.

The conversation starts with an investigation of love and intimate relationship (which is where many people experience pain and struggle) in the context of the spiritual search. Pointers are offered toward a transformation from the prison of codependency to the freedom of authentic relating, and toward the possibility of a new paradigm of enlightened relationship. The conversation continues with an investigation of whether health and well-being actually matter in spiritual liberation, and how pain, illness, and death can be met in awakened perception. Questions such as "Is there such a thing as cellular enlightenment?" and "Does caring for our planetary home become part of an awakened life?" are addressed here. The final part of the conversation investigates the role of work, money, and finding your true life's purpose. Often, these very earthly concerns are precisely the ones we've been told we should turn away from on the traditional spiritual path. Today, however, there's a new conversation happening that includes awakened action, what it means to be of service, the role of passion and joy in work, and transformation of the relationship to money. The new spirituality, arising from an evolutionary perspective, is unafraid of getting its hands dirty in the world of human affairs. And so, too, this book is unafraid to bring these once-taboo topics out into the open.

HOW TO READ THIS BOOK

You probably have already noticed that some terms (especially, *awakening* and *enlightenment*) are used interchangeably; and as you continue to read, you will come across many more interchangeable terms. This is not because I want to confuse you; although your mind *will* be confused if you attempt to decipher the words in a very literal way, or according to a specific spiritual tradition. Many spiritual words are burdened with layers of meaning accrued over millennia of indoctrination. *Enlightenment* is one of these words: historically, it has been used to describe an unattainable state of spiritual realization. I use it (interchangeably with the word *awakening*) to strip it of its heavy spiritual and intellectual heritage and to simply point to the realization of our true nature as wholeness when we awaken out of the dream of separation. *God* is another one of these words, weighed down by religious and cultural beliefs. I use this word occasionally (interchangeably with words such as *consciousness* or *beingness* or *life's intelligence*) to point to the dimension of formlessness that exists prior to form and gives birth to form.

But words themselves are not the truth; they are simply servants of the truth, and I use them to point to the inexpressible, to that which is beyond words. Some words you will be repelled by, others will deeply resonate with you. Take in what speaks to your inner knowing and discard the rest. Look beneath the form of the words to the essence of what is being spoken about. Allow the rhythm and the flow to carry you into the silent space between words.

You may also be perplexed by the apparent contradictions in some of the concepts talked about here. This book is not about facts or theory or knowledge. The scientific or historical references are there only to offer you a context for your awakening (and for the awakening of humanity). I adhere to no ideology or protocol, and there are no methods or techniques offered here. What I offer arises out of the untamable truth of direct inner experience.

ARE YOU WILLING TO SAY YES?

As you read the following pages, dear reader, allow the words to be like sparks that ignite your own awakening. (Or, if you are already on fire with that which is awake in you, then allow the words to fan the flame even higher.) Devote yourself to living the truth of this awakening—radically—in every aspect of your life.

Awakening calls us to the edge of who we think we are and challenges all our habitual responses to life. It's easier to turn away from this edge and stay in the comfort zone of our own limitation. The invitation is for you to stop running away and instead turn around and face this edge with an unadulterated yes.

Out of this yes, a new you will be born, a you that lives an authentically awakened life in which your actions are aligned with your true divine nature. And out of this new you, a new world will be born. It is unlikely that this world will be created overnight, as many New Age teachings propose. It is more likely to be built brick by brick—metaphorically and literally—as increasing numbers of people embody awakened consciousness. As old-world structures become obsolete and die and are replaced by social, cultural, political, and economic structures that reflect the highest expression of human potential, there's a high probability of great upheaval. Certainly, birth (whether it is the birth of a child or the birth of a new paradigm of consciousness) is messy and there is no guarantee of the outcome. But it's also inevitable. Once the contractions have begun, there is no going back.

With the possibility of the birth of a new world, it's also very possible that life as we know it completely destroys itself. Perhaps the quantum leap into a higher order necessitates the end of the current structures created within an old paradigm of consciousness. Perhaps humanity has to be totally obliterated before something new is born, like a phoenix from the ashes. There is no way to absolutely know. Although this book invites you into the collaboration with the evolution of consciousness, it's not about clinging to the hope of salvation. It's about being willing to open to the deepest truth of who you are, to live a radically awakened life … even if it means the end of "you" as who you think you are, and the end of "the world" as you believe it to be.

Despite the unknown and unforeseen challenges, are you willing to say *yes*? Are you willing to wholeheartedly embrace the possibility that this is the most exciting time to be alive? And that your awakening is the sole purpose of your life? If your answer is indeed a resounding affirmative, then this book will support you in the realization of true freedom and the fulfillment of a life lived in the infinite openness of this *yes*.

PART ONE

A NEW

CONSCIOUSNESS

AND A NEW WORLD

CHAPTER 1

Evolutionary Darkness and the Birth of Light

RADICAL TIMES

The story of humanity has been a cyclical one of war and peace. Looking back over several millennia, we see regular outbreaks of violence, cruelty, and war interspersed with short periods of relative harmony and stability. It has also been a story of innovation, breakthrough, and triumph. But as long as the unspeakable suffering of torture, slaughter, and starvation still exist, we cannot say this is a story of awakening.

Up until now, many of us in the West have been able to insulate ourselves from the horror of humanity's history. Not so long ago, we would read about the defeat and the victory of war in books, watch movies about the brutality of slavery, be shocked by the hidden corruption in governmental institutions, and be saddened to know that children were starving in some parts of the world; but none of this would really make any difference to our lives. Sheltered in our story of the "modern civilized world," we believed that these things happened to other people but not to us. For some of us in the West, our day-to-day reality has been one of safety, comfort, and security. Whatever dramas took place were for the most part contained in the crucible of our private lives, through divorce, bankruptcy, unexpected illness, or addiction. Today, however, the turmoil of life has escalated, and the drama has become a collective one.

When crisis is no longer something that happens to a stranger on the other side of the world but something very real that arrives on our doorstep, everything we know and everything we hold dear is rocked to the core. The global communications network now allows us to connect with people from all cultures, ages, and backgrounds in a way that we've never been able to before. People we've never seen or spoken with now mean something to us. We hear of their personal stories and we share in their gains and losses, their joys and heartbreaks. Today, what happens thousands of miles away is poignantly felt in our hearts. News of political, economic, corporate, social, and environmental systems on the verge of collapse reaches us in an instant. There is a growing awareness of the interconnectivity of things. And for some people, there's a growing awareness of the unprecedented shifts in the energetic structure of the earth and solar system, with a sensitivity to how these shifts may be impacting weather patterns as well as our health. Many long-established systems are crumbling, and it's likely that as we move through this century, many more external structures will do the same. It's a sign of profound change and is accompanied by the dissolution of many deeply held psychological structures.

Such radical times are calling into question the way we've been doing things. Obviously something isn't working. The insanity of man killing his fellow man and destroying his own habitat is testament to this. But something much deeper than "fixing what's wrong" needs to be addressed. We've been trying new ideas and new technologies for many hundreds of years and nothing has made a real difference. It's no longer serving us to take action without investigating what drives the momentum for this action. Some people are beginning to realize that no amount of external change will be effective; only an internal change will get to the root of the problem.

The problem lies deep within the human psyche, which has been hypnotized into viewing the world through the lens of separation. We have forgotten that our true nature is wholeness itself, and so we believe ourselves to be separate from one another, from the world, from the cosmos, and from God. This erroneous perception is the cause of all inner and outer conflict. If this error in perception is to be remedied, and if this remedy is to have any long-lasting impact, a total turnaround or revolution in human consciousness must take place.

The rumblings of this revolution are already being felt in the hearts and minds of many people. But if it is not yet awake in you, then it has not truly begun. You are at the leading edge of this revolution ... and nothing can change until *you* do. Your awakening out of the dream of separation, and the ensuing discovery of the wholeness of your essential nature and the wholeness of life itself, is the only real possibility to end suffering.

But for this discovery to be the source of real change in you—and the source of real change in the world—there needs to be an honest infusion of light through every detail of your life. In time, there will be an integration of this new consciousness that will give you fresh eyes through which to see the world. This is what is meant by *embodiment;* and without it, enlightenment remains at best a temporary spiritual state and at worst an intellectual pursuit. It's a common—and mistaken—belief that awakening leads to a life of perfection in which nothing painful happens. Many people think they are being spiritual just because they are feeling happy or grateful or ecstatic. What's really happening is that the river of life is flowing in a way that conforms to their idea of what it feels like to be spiritual.

Authentic awakening has nothing to do with the accumulation of good feelings or with identification with a role, albeit a spiritual one. It's not about being happy when things are going your way; it's about being anchored in the light of awareness, come what may. It's in the darkest moments that we get pulled by the archaic patterns of dysfunctional thinking. Authentic awakening says *yes* even to the darkness and has the compassion to meet what is truly here without denial or escapism or the attempt to fix it. The light within you, when resolutely recognized in all circumstances, has the capacity to embrace everything. This uncompromising acceptance is, in fact, your true nature. It is nothing less than the unbounded space of consciousness that is here, beneath and beyond the story of who you think you are. To deeply rest here is a new way of being. Whether the river flows gently or turbulently, to rest here means that something obsolete will die and a radically new way of living will be born.

A NEW EVOLUTIONARY IMPULSE

When a living system (any self-organizing structure that has a dynamic relationship with its environment) reaches maximum stress, it can respond in one of two ways: it can either descend into chaos or it can jump into a higher order. Some examples of these living systems are: biological systems (such as individual species), physiological systems (such as specific organs of the body), ecological systems (such as soil or the atmosphere), social systems (such as politics or the economy), cultural systems (such as art or philosophy), psychological systems (such as memory and emotions), and cosmic systems (such as planets, stars, and galaxies). There are many more examples of such systems to be found in both inner and outer space. Whatever form the living system takes, its primary concern is the maintenance of optimal function. It does this by fine-tuning a state of balance amid ever-changing conditions: this is called *homeostasis*. This delicate dance of equilibrium could potentially go on indefinitely, keeping things in a state of perpetual sameness, if it weren't for the hardwired impulse for increasing complexity, otherwise known as *growth*. Unlike mechanical or non-living systems, such as buildings or bicycles, living systems *interact* with their environment. There is an ongoing stimulus-response cycle that creates a pressure to adapt to the changing conditions. At some point, the demand of adaptation exceeds the capacity for homeostasis and the system experiences stress. This is a *bifurcation* moment: the road splits in two and, depending on a myriad of interconnecting factors, one of these roads is taken and a new destiny is carved out.

In biological systems, this is the point at which a species either becomes extinct or re-creates itself as a more complex and intelligent organism. We've seen this with the emergence of multi-celled organisms from a single cell, and with the development of Homo sapiens from primates. In social and cultural systems, this is when a structure either collapses or reorganizes itself as an expression of a more progressive society. An example of this is the rise of feminism at the end of the 19th century and how this led to an increase of women's political, economic, and sexual rights (at least in some parts of the world).

If we look at the living system of the human body, the bifurcation moment comes as a "healing crisis" when the body is sick. This is when physical symptoms intensify and either a more chronic condition sets in or the body's innate healing intelligence is activated. This often happens with the support of some kind of holistic treatment, and there's usually a miraculous return to wellness and sometimes a rise into a higher state of health.

If we look at the living system of the human psyche, this crisis point can be called an "emotional breakdown." It's when the normal capacity to respond to everyday situations is interrupted by overwhelming emotions. This "emotional breakdown" often happens due to a suppression of unwanted energies, which is likely to lead to anxiety attacks and more extreme states of mind. The other possible response to this "emotional breakdown" is a gentle opening to what has been previously unmet on a feeling level. This opening is usually supported by some kind of counselor, with a resultant purging of emotional baggage that allows for a more conscious relationship to life.

A crisis of an even deeper dimension of the human spirit is sometimes called a "dark night of the soul." It is experienced as an existential abandonment that can lead to either a sense of alienation and isolation from other people and from the world; or, a surrender into the abyss of nothingness and a "coming home" to the all-embracing oneness of being. In all instances—biological, physical, psychological, or spiritual—conditions appear to worsen before there is the possibility of breakthrough to a whole new level of well-being. And in all cases, some kind of intelligent intervention is part of the healing journey.

While this is a very brief look at a complex situation, perhaps you can get a sense of how each crisis point is a catalyst for growth. Maybe this has already been your personal experience. At some point or another everyone experiences crisis in their lives. However, this is not always consciously recognized, and the opportunity for growth is missed. We often think that when things get challenging there is something wrong. But challenge, or stress, is an evolutionary driver that serves the creative unfoldment of existence.

Out of the primordial emptiness, the process of life keeps unfolding. The formless gives birth to form, always becoming more of itself. Existence continually seeks more ways to express itself. Ever since what we may call "the beginning of time," there has been an exponential rise in the complexity and permutations of life-forms. In humanity, this evolutionary impulse expresses itself as the urge to procreate and the desire to manifest more possibilities and variations of everything. In other words, it's the impulse to produce more, to have more, to learn more, to explore, to expand, to improve, and to grow. It's the driving force behind all artistic creativity, technological innovation, scientific discovery, and social change. It's also the underlying cause of overpopulation, resource depletion, environmental pollution, and the development of ever-bigger weapons of mass destruction.

Evolution is driven by a *yes*-mechanism. It gives rise to all creations, even those that are destructive. This *yes* is unconditional. It says *yes* to all births and all deaths. It says *yes* to all acts of genius, as well as *yes* to all acts of stupidity. The act of creation allows everything; it does not differentiate between good and bad. As positive and negative polarities reach a peak, there is a collision that forces a bifurcation point. At this point in our evolution, humanity has arrived at this same fork in the road. We are faced with either total annihilation or a quantum leap into a new future.

Despite appearances, we are now perfectly poised for a giant evolutionary step forward and upward. Collectively and individually, we are being given the opportunity for an upgrade. Contrary to our conventional way of seeing things, the darkness we perceive in the world and the darkness we experience in our lives is here to serve us. The pain and horror is the grit in the oyster that makes the pearl: it's the catalyst for evolution. When life comes crashing down around us, it's so hard to believe that the darkness isn't an indicator of something gone terribly wrong. But this is not necessarily the deeper truth of the matter. Often, in fact, it is a sign that there's something wonderfully right. It shows us that the dawn of a new light is emerging.

As we stand at the precipice of an exciting transition, we have a choice. We either collapse in the face of our challenges or we do something radical. The former is familiar to us; it's what we've done for millennia. When faced with potential danger, our automatic response is "fight or flight." And when danger becomes prolonged and the hope of a brighter future fades away, we collapse into fear and despair. If we are to evolve, as individuals and as a species, a new response is required. Instead of fight or flight, we're called to turn around and join forces with evolution itself by saying *yes* to that which is dying and *yes* to that which is emerging. Even though it appears as if the outer world of form is breaking down, it's the inner world of consciousness that has reached a crisis point.

The invitation and the possibility for you, and each of us, is to allow your world to be rocked, to let it all come crashing down, to be willing to be stripped bare of all that you think you have and all that you think you are. In losing every notion, every image, every concept that has upheld a sense of "me" and "mine"—and this may or may not include the loss of every material thing you think you own—you discover that which can never be lost, that which is immovable and invulnerable to change.

EVOLVING BEYOND EGO

We've spent lifetimes as humans and as more primitive life forms reacting to stimuli. As biological organisms, we are hard-wired for survival. Not only do we seek out food and shelter—and at times comfort and pleasure—we also will do anything to protect ourselves from danger. The fight or flight response is embedded in our genes. When faced with a threat—and there are many in the natural world—we either resist it by fighting it or we avoid it by fleeing from it. There's nothing wrong with this. It's an in-built mechanism that has served us for millions of years. It's part of our heritage. It allows us to navigate the world of form and without it we would not be alive as a species today. Because animals and plants have not yet developed the capacity for self-reflection, this automatic fight or flight response remains a purely biological function. It's a natural reaction that serves the immediate needs of the life form. We could even say it is an innocent behavior. In other words, it is not contaminated by a sense of personal ownership.

In humans, the gift of self-awareness has given us access to an inner dimension in which not only are we aware of ourselves as defined by physical form (the body), but we're also aware of ourselves as defined by psychological forms (thoughts, sensations, feelings, perception of time, emotions, and memories). It is this *identification* with both physical and psychological forms that has come to be known as the ego: the body has become "*my* body," thoughts are "*my* thoughts," feelings are "*my* feelings," and so on. Since all forms are born into duality, "my body" is either a beautiful body or an ugly body, "my thoughts" are either positive thoughts or negative thoughts, "my feelings" are either pleasurable feelings or painful feelings, and so on. Not only do we take ownership of these forms, but we also confuse them with who we are. They become a part of the "*me.*" This "*me*" is what we refer to when we say, "I am beautiful," "I am ugly," "I am happy," or "I am sad." This is how we get lost in our personal story. And it is this story that is the source of our sense of separation.

There is an even deeper inner dimension, beyond form; one that could be called the spiritual dimension of formlessness, where we can become aware of awareness itself. There is a stillness and a silence there that is the source of peace. It is also the source of higher human qualities, such as compassion, kindness, forgiveness, gratitude, and generosity. But even these more enlightened expressions of life are often taken ownership of by the ego. Beliefs about ourselves, such as "I am compassionate," "I am kind," "I am forgiving," "I am grateful," or "I am generous," can easily become additional layers to our story. Because we invest so much in our story, our whole sense of self is derived from it. The upholding of our story becomes something we must defend at all costs. And so starts the war, both within and without.

The process of disidentification with our story and recognizing that there is a ground of being beneath and beyond all forms is the birth of awakening. Yet still, for the majority of people, this recognition has not yet happened, and the ego and its sense of separate self is the primary driving engine for all inner and outer activity.

Ego is a word much bandied about these days, and there's some confusion as to its meaning. Psychologists refer to the ego as something we need to strengthen in order to have a healthy sense of self, healthy relationships, and a healthy interaction with the everyday world. Metaphysical and spiritual teachings refer to the ego as something erroneous or even evil that needs to be obliterated if we are to transcend suffering and selfishness. And many people believe that the ego is some kind of "thing" or entity, perhaps located somewhere in the brain. But has anyone ever found the ego? Does the ego actually exist? And can you actually get rid of it?

A certain degree of inquiry is likely to reveal that the ego is not a tangible thing. Rather, it is an "inner experience," a process of mental activity with both a *relative* and an *absolute* dimension to it. On the relative level, a healthy sense of self or ego is indeed necessary if you are to successfully make decisions and take actions. The ego at this level acts as a kind of navigation system, informing you of danger so that you can avoid damage to the life-form that you express yourself through. The benefit of this on a physical level is obvious, and there's also a psychological benefit. Without an ego you would be unable to differentiate between *you* and *me,* and what is *in* you and what is *outside* of you—unable to relate to anyone or to the world in a way that's meaningful and useful. This could be called a state of psychosis. Obviously, the ego and its sense of "I" serves a vital purpose. But on an absolute level, believing yourself to actually *be* the ego is a hindrance to awakening to the truth of who you are.

These two seemingly opposing views of ego are not neces-sarily mutually exclusive—truth is paradoxical. The relative and the absolute exist as two sides of the same coin, and the relationship between them is significant when it comes to living an authentically awakened life in today's world. In the context of liberation from suffering, the ego is nothing more than a conglomeration of habitual thought patterns and subsequent behavior patterns that revolve around the protection of a sense of "*me*" and "*mine*." In itself, this is harmless and a necessary aspect of living as form. And yet, this "*me*" conglomerate has become a powerful force that runs our lives, most often with a detrimental result.

The momentum of millions of years of survival has created a kind of "out of control" entity that is counterproductive not only to our highest potential, but also to our very existence. Without an awareness of who we really are, humanity is heading toward destruction. The rising incidence of physical, emo-tional, and mental dysfunction we see in society, the escalating greed and corruption within long-established institutions and corporations, and the intensification of religious and political wars are all evidence of our allegiance to ego. Why does the ego have so much power in our lives? And why has this situa-tion gone on for so long? The answer lies in the dynamics of living systems: The ego keeps itself alive by maintaining a homeostatic state. It does this by adopting the fight or flight mechanism for its own self-serving agenda.

Whenever the ego feels psychologically threatened, it reacts either by going to war or by seeking safety, just as it would if the physical form was threatened. Going to war is arguing with reality. You don't like what's happening because it doesn't conform to what you think *should* be happening. You don't like what someone said to you. You don't like the way life's turned out. You feel angry, sad, confused, despondent, or bad. If these thoughts and emotions do not conform to your image of yourself as powerful, successful, happy, lucky, or spiritual, you resist them and argue with life. This argument takes place whenever you blame your mother, your father, your partner, your child, your boss, your friend, or the person working behind the shop counter for your feelings of discomfort and pain. It also happens when you blame the government, the economy, the planetary alignments, or the weather.

Blame and its many offshoots, such as anger, resentment, bitterness, and self-righteousness, are defensive strategies designed to protect you from harm. But what's really happening is that this conglomerate of thoughts and emotions we call the ego is keeping itself alive for its own sake. Without the attempt to resist the stark-naked truth of what's unfolding in your experience, ego's grip would weaken. We could say, in this case, that the ego would die, but what really dies is the *investment* in ego. In its place would be an awakened presence that cuts through all stories to an unbounded acceptance. But until the time comes when you're ready to take this leap into the wide-open vista of clear-seeing, your investment in egoic identification keeps you hostage in the dream of duality. *I'm right, you're wrong* is the ego's mantra, and adherence to this mantra is the cause of both personal and global suffering.

Once we pay attention to the ego's primary strategy of going to war, it's easy to see the reactive posturing that runs our lives. However, it's less easy to see the ego's secondary strategy of seeking safety, since it comes in many guises that don't conform to the popular idea of ego as arrogant, pompous, or overconfident. When you seek safety you stay in your comfort zone, psychologically running away from what scares you and running toward what gratifies you. But staying in the comfort zone is far from comfortable in the truest sense; it's comfortable because it's habitual.

The ego abhors change of any kind. Whether change comes in the form of calamity or opportunity, it's a threat to the image of self that the ego has constructed. Perhaps your husband, wife, or lover has left you and you are bereft. Do you retreat into thinking you're unlovable or unworthy because somehow you've come to believe that this is who you are? Or do you gently open to the grief of loss and allow yourself to be moved beyond looking for love in another to knowing *yourself* as the love that you seek? Perhaps you have a dream to write a book, start a business, or travel around the world, but every time you take a step toward this dream you feel incredible internal resistance or circumstances appear to be against you. Do you put the dream on the back burner? Do you give up and believe it's not your fate? Or do you softly open to the call to deepen your relationship to life? Are you willing to open to a new conversation that takes you beyond conditioned reactions?

You can recognize ego's comfort zone by becoming aware of the voices in your head saying *if*, *but*, and *maybe*. It's the voice that makes excuses, the voice of procrastination, or the voice of doubt, but it's also the voice of hope. Hope, while a vital lifeline in extreme situations, such as in the concentration camps of the Holocaust or being stranded on Mount Everest in a blizzard, is mostly ego's ploy to prevent change. It is the "one-day syndrome." For example, you may say to yourself: *One day I will find my soul mate*, *One day I will be happy and rich*, or *One day I will be enlightened*. This is the seeking mechanism in disguise. The problem is that the "one day" never comes, because hope is based on a dream of future salvation. Real salvation lies in saving yourself from the tyranny of your own thinking, and this requires rising above ego's strategies.

What was once an innocent mechanism that served us in terms of physical survival—and still does—has become corrupted by the voracious psychological appetite for a sense of "me" and "mine." Ego's fight or flight strategy is the antithesis of freedom. The continual reactivity to external and internal stimuli creates a deep discomfort we call stress. Examine this stress closely and you'll notice a restlessness that drives the momentum for all seeking. Whether the search is for material or spiritual satisfaction, this seeking still prevents you from knowing yourself as the pure beingness that underlies all forms. It's no wonder that stress has become synonymous with the modern condition. The challenge today is to grow beyond this outmoded survival mechanism. It's time to evolve beyond ego.

THE WORLD IS AS WE SEE IT

We do not see the world as it *is*, but as we *believe* it to be. When we first come into this world there is a freshness to our experience. Every feeling, sensation, and movement of energy is new. Without words, concepts, or memories, we meet this uncharted territory with totality. We see things as they really are. Everything is created equal in our eyes. The division between good and bad, right and wrong has not yet started.

With time, however, the original, transparent lens of innocent seeing is inevitably tainted. We learn that some things physically and emotionally hurt and the ancient survival mechanism kicks in. We label what hurts as "not love," and we turn away to find the image of love we have created elsewhere. We feel scared, alone, vulnerable, incomplete, and we seek the safety and security of wholeness outside of ourselves. We forget that we *are* this love and that we are already whole. We manufacture an elaborate theory of who we think we are based on a mistaken identity. We forget that life *is* an expression of this love, that it is always perfectly whole as it is. Instead, we paint a picture of life based on an erroneous perception.

Your likes, dislikes, hopes, and fears are shaped by the unique story of your incarnation on earth. Your story includes the stories of your parents and family members, the story of your education, class, and religion, the planetary alignments at the moment you were born, and the historical era you are born into. All these stories weave a tapestry of beliefs that color the world we see, yet we claim that what we see is reality. This is the inevitability of personal and cultural conditioning.

The projection of this reality onto the world is the dream most people live in. Whether this dream is a nightmare or a fairy tale, it is of your own making. Whether it is a story of happiness or sadness, success or failure, purpose or purposelessness, or blessing or punishment, is up to you. For a vast majority of people, the story revolves around a sense of being a victim: a belief that someone or something is to blame for your suffering. All personal strategies of attack and defense stem from an ignorance of who you really are. The majority of humanity consistently fails to rise into the majesty of its true nature. Instead, we have succumbed to a belief that we are separate from one another, separate from life, and separate from the *one being* that animates the whole of existence.

It's no surprise, then, that our collective reality is a reflection of millions of stories of lack, limitation, struggle, and seeking. The greed, competitiveness, cruelty, and conflict we see in the world are a direct result of our state of consciousness. Our actions are a consequence of our internal reality; and it's our actions that create our external reality. Whatever is unilluminated, incomplete, or unfinished in *you* is what is unilluminated, incomplete, and unfinished in the world. Whatever is toxic, polluted, or corrupted in *you* is what is toxic, polluted, and corrupted in the world. It is a common belief that heaven and hell exist as real places, somewhere we go to when we die, depending on how good or bad we are. But heaven and hell are right here inside *you*.

Hell is what happens when you are lost in the identification with physical and psychological form and claim ownership of your thoughts and feelings. When you believe your story to be the truth, even if the story is a fairy tale with a happy ending, it is still hell. It's hell because anything that can be clutched by the ego is destined to die, and this includes every form, idea, imagination, and hope. Unless you recognize the luminosity of what remains when everything dies, you will still be caught in the dream.

Heaven is what happens when you awaken out of this dream. It is the recognition that the world has no meaning other than the meaning you assign to it. This is not to say that you live in a meaningless world: the belief in "a meaningless world," if unexamined, remains a notion of the mind. The recognition that your beliefs about the world are not the truth but, rather, conditioned mental and emotional responses based on the past and projected into the future, is the beginning of clear seeing. When this recognition first takes place, there is a tendency to turn away from these thoughts and emotions. Paradoxically, it's the turning around to meet these thoughts and emotions that offers the genuine possibility of liberation.

This meeting, when executed with a gracious openness, is a sincere inquiry into what is really here. It's a laser-beam sword of awareness that cuts the cord of suffering. Pain, whether it be physical or emotional, is experienced *as it is,* not as a story of pain. When we don't follow the thoughts that wrap themselves around the experience of pain, or label the pain as "manageable," "unbearable," or "life-destroying," what we call pain can be fully met without the baggage of the past and without agenda for the future.

This opening to present-moment experience, when conducted with the conscious surrender of a wave-surfer, leads you into the nakedness of absolute reality. It's a vertical investigation (a movement of consciousness as it moves away from linear thinking) into the nature of thinking and feeling that reveals the truth that all thoughts, feelings, and sensations are temporary. Much as you try, you cannot hold on to them, control them, or even stop them. Each day, each hour, and each minute is filled with hundreds, if not thousands, of thoughts, feelings, and sensations. If you take a pause and bring your attention gently into the present moment, you may notice that every thought, feeling, and sensation rises and falls, just like a wave on the ocean. If you are very still and silent inside, you may notice the space in between all the waves. Awakening is the discovery of that which is still here and unchanging even when thoughts and feelings change.

THE PARADOX OF REALITY

Many spiritual seekers, and even spiritual teachers, who've experienced the absolute truth of emptiness believe the world is an illusion. Certain proponents of the new physics support this view by stating that the physical world—including things such as chairs, cars, computers, animals, plants, and even your body—is not real but a projection of the mind. It's a belief that is prevalent particularly in nondual and metaphysical teachings.

Initially, this new perspective can liberate you from the drama of life, so that you stop taking things so personally, and this feels like a kind of freedom. But if you continue to invest your sense of peace in this belief that the world is an illusion, it can easily become a veneer with the appearance of enlightenment. With time, however, this veneer ossifies and becomes another layer of egoic identity.

The attempt to transcend the world and its messiness often leads to an "existential numbness" that is mistaken for spiritual liberation. What's really going on here is a denial of full engagement with life, and an avoidance of intimately meeting the depth and breadth of feeling that arises in response to the vicissitudes of our human experience. There's no real freedom in an "I'm enlightened so nothing can touch me" attitude. The escape from the prison of identification with physical and psychological form is replaced by the less obvious bondage of "spiritual detachment." This so-called detachment is actually a new kind of attachment: the story of "I am beautiful/ugly/successful/a failure/happy/sad/Christian/Buddhist" is replaced by the story of "I am nothing." It's a retreat into the perfection of an inner world in which the horror of the outer world has no place. It's a rejection of any internal state that doesn't match your mental picture of a spiritual life. There's no real peace in this, but a subtle and pernicious war that perpetuates both inner and outer conflict.

The refusal of suffering results in a kind of coldness, a non-acceptance of the vulnerability of being truly alive as a human being. On a behavioral level, this reveals itself in a number of ways. For some, there's an avoidance of relationship and its capacity to break us apart, to strip us of our defenses, and to touch us in the most tender of places. For others, there's an abdication of self-care and self-responsibility that can lead to excessive risk-taking or even harmful lifestyle choices. In these cases, people often feel that if the body is not real, why not push it to its limits, and why should they care about the strength of their heart, the longevity of their kidneys, or whether they're overweight. For others, there's a lack of concern for sentient life. They may believe that if the world and everything in it is an illusion, that they don't need to care what happens to the Jews, the Iraqis, the polar bears, the honeybees, the polluted rivers, or the depleted soil. What is revealed in this kind of refusal of suffering is an absence of the compassion that is a natural extension of true awakening. It's a compassion that arises not out of moral obligation, but out of the fragrance of an awakened heart. Compassion is awakeness meeting itself in the heart of everything. It's about embracing both the dark and the light and finding the freedom that is there within it all.

The discovery of true freedom requires you to surrender your concepts of nonduality, spirituality, or enlightenment, and to meet life with innocent eyes. This innocent seeing is an open inquiry into what's here right now in your immediate and direct experience. It requires you to stop investing in your personal story, whether it is a story of victimhood or transcendence. This noninvestment is not a denial of suffering. It's not an insulation from the heartbreak of witnessing horrific acts of violence, injustice, and cruelty; nor is it a repression of anger, fear, despair, and grief. But it *is* an end to the ownership of thoughts and emotions that perpetuate the story of suffering. It is an end to the story of separation. The experience of pain or terror *as it is* without trying to fix, control, get rid of, or justify it puts an end to the suffering of "poor me" and stops the war between us and them, right and wrong, or good and bad.

To reject your direct experience of life is not only a continuation of the conflict inherent in the story of suffering (which we attempt to heal through our spiritual endeavors), it's also a kind of madness. The experience of "something happening" is a continual unfoldment within our perceptual field. We see colors, shapes, and patterns. We hear sounds that scare us and sounds that soothe us. We even hear the sound of silence. We smell things that repel us and things that attract us. We taste all manner of horrible and delightful things. We feel the sun on our skin, the moisture of a lover's kiss, and the stab of the dentist's injection. It is clearly not the world itself that is an illusion: as long as you are here to experience the world, it exists. Rather, it is the story you impose upon the world that is not real.

Reality requires us to see things from a whole new perspective that embraces the crazy paradox of life. And it is this all-inclusive perspective that is emerging today as the cutting edge of spiritual inquiry. As more people turn their attention to spiritual awareness as a way to find peace and freedom amid an increasingly insane world, new questions are being asked. Spiritual seekers today want to know how awakening is lived in the midst of everyday life. What happens to our personality if we have evolved beyond ego? And what happens to the world if we are free of suffering?

So many of us have inherited a transcendent view of spirituality in which there is a split between the divine and the human. This divisive perspective is deeply embedded in traditional religious and spiritual teachings, for which renouncing the world is paramount if we are to become more godly, as well as in more recent New Age teachings in which ascending to a better world is the goal. This is a sign of the domination of egoic mind and its primary mechanism of separation.

Perhaps as a way to heal the split between heaven and earth, a new spiritual frequency is emerging that embraces our humanity and allows topics traditionally excluded from the spiritual dimension to be included in the exploration of what it means to be fully awake in today's world. This more holistic perspective is the natural domain of the sacred feminine. But this isn't just a return of an ancient feminine way; rather, it's a refined and evolved feminine energy that speaks to each of us as individuals about our role in humanity's awakening. This new spiritual frequency is very possibly changing the face of modern spirituality.

CHAPTER 2

The Feminine Face
of Awakening

IS AWAKENESS BEYOND GENDER?

In many spiritual circles, it is unpopular to explore the feminine face of awakening. Certainly, from a nondual perspective, it's convenient to completely avoid any dialogue that refers to the role of the feminine in spirituality. And so there's a tendency, in some of the more philosophical or intellect-based spiritual teachings, for language to be neutral or conceptual, and this can lead to a certain dryness.

On the other hand, in more earth-based spiritual teachings, the pendulum swings the other way, and there is a passionate expression of the feminine as the goddess archetype, with the emphasis on the sensual and the emotional dimension of life. When this impassioned feminine arises as a reaction to the traditional spiritual emphasis on transcendence and detachment, there can be a forgetting of the necessity to be rooted in stillness before moving into the world with her myriad manifestations. If the inner transformation has not happened, then ego continues to play itself out, and, in some goddess-based circles, this leads to a kind of feminism that excludes and divides itself against the deep silent core of consciousness. This subtle inner division ends up as a distortion of the true sacred feminine if it is not attended to consciously.

Awakeness itself is genderless. The luminous truth shines equally brightly in all beings. And certainly, as has been my own experience, the *superficial* expression of masculine and feminine traits often recedes into the background and may even dissolve when one awakens to that which is beyond gender. When identity is no longer derived from physical and psychological form, the upholding of many gender-based behaviors becomes obsolete. This does not mean you become sexless, neutral, or bland. On the contrary, you become more whole and balanced.

Although awakeness is singular and without gender, there's also a naïveté in trying to deny the mystery of duality as it dances through form. The Tao of life undeniably expresses itself as the polarity of masculine-feminine. Without this, there would be no creation. But these polarities are so much more than any inherited idea we have of what this looks like. They are more than role-defined responses or any historical image handed down to us by religion, culture, or tradition. In awakening, you not only transcend all gender-based stereotypes, you also become a conduit for the dance of masculine and feminine energies to play out their fullness through you. Once again, this is the beautiful and crazy paradox of awake reality!

The invitation here is to listen beyond the convention of words to the source from which all words arise. It is here, in the silence of being, that the real essence of what we call masculine and feminine can be heard. The true nature of both the masculine and the feminine is essential to the existence of life. Even the big bang is an expression of the marriage of masculine-feminine polarities. Consider the possibility that before existence was born, there was an endless and timeless emptiness. And out of this deep dimension of empty beingness arose a singular moment. We could call this the moment of conception or "the impulse to become," where the totality of creation spilled out through time and space and even now is continuing to proliferate in all its multiplicity. The penetrative quality of *beingness*, which we could also call *presence*, is the essence of all manifestations. It is the masculine "seed of life." The proliferating quality of *becomingness*, which we could also call *radiance* (as in radiating out to include everything), is what we see as the organic expression of all life forms. It is the feminine "birth of life."

In nature, the expression of masculine and feminine remain untainted by any mental or emotional interpretations. There is a purity to a rose, a caterpillar, an oak tree, or a kitten. Each of these is fully present as itself and radiant with the fullness of life. In nature, there is no ego, just the simplicity of existence. In humanity, the masculine and feminine have become tainted by egoic identification with the surface form, and so we end up with all sorts of notions and dogmatic beliefs about what it means to be a man or a woman. Most often there's an emphasis on the emotional and intellectual differences between men and women, and this leads to the battle of the sexes that we see exaggerated and glamorized in the media and in the entertainment industry. Even the exploration of the more sacred aspects of the masculine and the feminine is distorted by socially, culturally, and personally colored beliefs.

The new spiritual frequency arising today may have the look and feel of a feminine vibration, but it actually has nothing to do with gender; rather, it is about something much more universal. It is actually a frequency and expression that can come through a female or a male body, or through any life form. While the feminine capacity to give birth to something new, including the innate impulse to cocreate, collaborate, and nurture, is more easily expressed in women due to their biological ability to give birth to a new life, it's also an impulse that is latent in each of us, regardless of gender. Today, this frequency is available to both women and men as a *psychological* birthing that is happening on a personal and planetary level. We are giving birth to a new consciousness that wholeheartedly embraces the transient yet undeniable reality of the human experience within the infinite ocean of awakeness. It's a love affair between earth and heaven that has the potential to give birth to a radically new world in which each of us is, metaphorically, both the "mother" and the "child."

As the mother, each one of us is called to embody an inner steadfastness in the face of the unknown, an unflappable groundedness in the midst of chaos, an unconditional acceptance of the movement of life that includes birth, death, and everything in between, and an unshakable faith in the sacredness of life in all its expressions. As the child, each one of us is called to embody a soft-bellied innocence, a fresh-eyed perspective rooted in present-moment awareness, a vibrant embrace of the unfolding nature of present-moment experience, and an unstoppable vision of humanity's infinite potential. Whether you are a mother, a father, a man, or a woman, young or old, you embody the archetypes of both "mother" and "child." We could also call these the qualities of *being* and *becoming* ... and they are alive in *you* right now, in this very moment. As you come to recognize this aliveness within, you will discover a power that can move mountains and create universes.

THE MIRACLE OF BIRTH AND THE POWER OF COLLABORATION

The miracle of giving birth to something new, of creating form out of emptiness, would not be possible without the willingness to say *yes*. *Yes* is a powerful statement, rooting us in the "I am–ness" of manifest reality and calling forth new life. It's also a sacred statement, because it heals all separation by holding the play of duality in the unconditional heart of this moment as it unfolds.

The female body is the perfect expression of this *yes*, holding deep within its cellular matrix the seed of consciousness ready to reveal itself through matter. A pregnant woman does not have to *do* anything in order to give birth. She does not need to impose her will; she just needs to be willing. Being naturally receptive, her body is designed to open and allow birth to take place. The more she relaxes and opens, the less painful or traumatic and often the more ecstatic the birth process can become. A woman has the innate capacity to surrender to an infinitely more intelligent and powerful force than her own mind.

This is the opposite of what we've been taught by the patriarchal mind-set that dominates society. It is also the opposite of the way the ego functions. Based on a paradigm of separation, both the world and the ego teach us to be competitive, defensive, and self-gratifying. We're conditioned to control our environment in order to get what we want and to feel safe. At the same time, millions of years of suppression have led us to subjugate our own intuitive knowing to an external authority, whether it be to a doctor, a priest, a politician, or a voice in our heads (the superego). This is the masculine way of hierarchy. And, of course, everything has its place, as can be seen in the expression of nature. Nevertheless, the lopsided emphasis on hierarchy, power, and control has created trouble in our minds, in our hearts, and in the world.

The feminine way is naturally attuned to the way of equality and collaboration. A woman holds the wisdom of interconnectedness. It's a visceral sense that arises from the simple and magnificent fact that a new life can grow in her womb that is inseparable from her own life. And she instinctively understands that relationship is the basis of life on earth, for as long as we exist in the world of form, we're in relationship to everything that exists. These qualities are a part of motherhood. Although the innate intelligence of being a mother has been obscured by layers of conditioning for many women, most women do not have to learn how to be a mother. A mother who still has her innate mothering instinct intact will love her child unconditionally, will devote herself to nurturing and protecting her child, and will sacrifice her own desires, and even her own life, to make sure this child survives and thrives.

As the new feminine frequency emerges into the consciousness of humanity and expresses itself through individuals, society, and culture, there's a shift from being blindly willful to being willing to collaborate. This new frequency is also showing up in the spiritual domain. These days, more than ever before, there's an intensification of the evolutionary process that compels us to consciously collaborate in waking up out of the dream of separation. Perhaps it's gradually dawning on us that the dissolution of egoic identification and the ensuing discovery of our underlying true nature might well be the answer to our global problems, and that spiritual liberation and earthly affairs are not in opposition to each other. Could it be that one day we may come to realize that being spiritual is nothing more and nothing less than being fully human? And could it be that enlightenment has nothing to do with transcending the world, but everything to do with bringing the full light of our divinity into the world? It is this kind of conversation that is currently taking us to the leading edge of spiritual inquiry and calling forth a new kind of spiritual leadership.

THE ROLE OF WOMEN IN SPIRITUAL LEADERSHIP

Historically, enlightenment has been a male arena. Until quite recently, there have been very few reports of women having attained enlightenment, and even fewer have taken up the role of spiritual teacher or spiritual leader. The inhibition of the feminine, in both spiritual and secular life, has left us with a masculine model of enlightenment in which the guru (almost always a male figure, metaphorically and often literally) sits on a pedestal without getting his hands dirty in the world of human affairs. Most of us have this model imprinted in our psyches to some degree or another, whether it be handed down by Western religion or by Eastern philosophy; Christian, Islamic, Hindu, and Buddhist spiritual teachings are dominated by male deities, prophets, and enlightened masters. Other than a few lesser-known female saints, women have traditionally been confined to their role within the family and community as child-bearer, cook, cleaner, and general homemaker. In some cultures women have been, and still are, regarded as the property of men. It is no wonder that women have had little say in the realm of spirituality up until this point in time.

Today, as the feminine face of awakening reveals itself, many of these archaic ideologies and hierarchical structures

45

are dissolving, and many more ordinary women are awakening and making themselves available for the role of spiritual leadership. But this feminine leadership has a different flavor than the masculine version. It has nothing to do with sitting on the guru seat, nor with adhering to spiritual doctrine. And neither does it deny the messiness of being human. Feminine leadership flows from the unconditional heart. It carries an innate purity that cuts through dogma. Today's female spiritual teachers aren't interested in an intellectual debate that upholds an enlightened perspective. And they do not adhere to any prescribed way of speaking about awakening. (This is often the case in certain spiritual circles that do adhere to prescribed ways, where there's an unspoken "code of conduct" in the language being used.) Instead, these new female spiritual teachers express a more fluid and juicy language that reflects the embodiment of awakening as a living human reality.

Many of today's spiritual teachers are ordinary women living modern lives, often with husbands, children, homes, and the usual everyday tasks to attend to. They look and dress just like you. They drive cars, clean the sink, go shopping, take care of their aging parents, and walk their dog. Many are also healers, therapists, practitioners, or facilitators of some kind. Awakening is often described by these women as a gentle unfoldment rather than a sudden explosion. However, there is no rule about how one awakens; it can happen in all sorts of ways. These spiritual teachers also speak of how ordinary life continues just as it was before, but with a deeper texture and a freedom from the burden of their story. It seems that many women are now gently yet insistently debunking many of the myths of enlightenment and showing us that awakening is accessible to each of us.

Of course, it's not just women who are inviting the embodiment of awakening, but also male teachers in whom awakening has matured in heart, body, and mind. The modern-day spiritual teacher (whether female or male) is called to embody the totality of being human, while at the same time recognizing the divine light at the core of it all. To be this light amid the darkness of the world is easier for women, simply because it is in a woman's nature. There is a selflessness to a woman's natural state, due to their physiological and psychological capacities to give birth and to nurture life. Unlike the male psyche, which is less attuned to the rhythms of nature, the female psyche has less of a need for lifetimes of ascetic practices to strip away the rigidity of egoic thinking. Of course, the female psyche has also been polluted by millennia of patriarchal domination, and the majority of women still suffer from deep confusion, anxiety, and ignorance of their true nature. But there are a growing number of women who are awake to the light of truth that lives within them, and these are the new leaders emerging in response to our increasing urgent need to heal and purify the earth and the world.

Many of these newly awakened individuals are already expressing this light through their actions. Many of them are still children, or at least young adults, such as environmental activist Severn Cullis-Suzuki, who at the age of twelve made her first international appearance at the Rio Earth Summit in 1992. And many of them are born into repressive regimes, but are stepping forward fearlessly to make a stand for right action, to redress the horrific imbalance and injustice within such areas as education, marriage, work, and freedom of speech, such as Malala Yousafzai, who won the Nobel Peace Prize in 2014 for her role in supporting women's education in Pakistan.

Without concern for personal consequence, these women are expressing and embodying the living light of truth in a totally practical way—for the benefit of all beings. These women do not need teachers, for they are already attuned to the innate wisdom of their innermost true nature.

You, too, on the deepest level, no matter your gender, are already inseparable from your innermost nature. The willingness to stop following the movement of the mind, to be fully *here now* in this and every moment, gives you access to the wisdom of life. It's a wisdom that has nothing to do with the thinking mind or knowledge, or with what has been passed down as wisdom through the ages, or even with anything you read here. It is the wisdom of *you,* because you *are* life.

Pause here for a moment, and listen with your innermost being. The invitation offered here—in the space between the words—is to the most precious discovery of your true nature. It's always here waiting for you to reclaim it, so that the light of your inherent wisdom can change your world from the inside out.

PART TWO

FULLY AWAKE AND

FULLY HUMAN

CHAPTER 3

The Shedding of Egoic Identification

THE INNER REVOLUTION

As increasing numbers of people report "awakening experiences," there is often confusion about what it means to be fully awake and fully human. Much of what is handed down as spiritual wisdom, even in today's spiritual circles, is an outdated perspective that does not speak to the totality of a sophisticated modern-day psyche. With the modern-day spiritual culture of hopping from one teacher to another, and the general melting pot of teachings available on the Internet, there's a tendency for myth making about how awakening is experienced and lived. If awakening is to be more than just a state that comes and goes, if it is to be an ongoing reality with a very real impact on your everyday world, then a more accurate arrow of inquiry must penetrate your mind and heart in order to anchor the truth in your gut.

For spiritual liberation to be fully actualized through every aspect of your humanity, and for it to give birth to a new you and a new world, awakening has to take root at the core of your being. A complete inner revolution of consciousness must take place before any real change in your inner or your outer world can become a reality. For this, your attention must be given with undying allegiance to the discovery of your innermost truth. It's a turning within that doesn't require you to renounce the world by living in seclusion on a mountaintop, but it does require you to surrender the need to control, possess, or worship anything in the world of form, whether it be a material accolade, a cherished belief, or a hope of salvation.

So much of our attention is taken up by wanting things to be other than the way they are. There's nothing wrong with wanting to grow beyond our limitations, improve our personal circumstances, or to make the world a better place to live in. This wanting is driven by the innate impulse to evolve. The problem arises when we attempt to fix, control, or eradicate things from an unilluminated perspective. There's no evidence that using the same state of mind that created an unwelcome situation to change that same situation is an effective strategy. And yet this is what most of humanity has been doing throughout history.

All we have to do is take an honest look at the world to see that a divided mind, or what A Course in Miracles[1] calls the "unholy mind," is a mind that does not know itself as wholeness. This quality of mind can only see through the lens of division and then make decisions based on this view. Whether it's the war against poverty, the war against crime, or the war against cancer, the way of war clearly doesn't work, because war cannot create peace. The idea of an enemy or something bad or evil that lurks "out there" and needs to be vanquished only serves to perpetuate war. As long as we are certain that what we *agree* with is worthy of love while what we *disagree* with should be condemned by hatred, conflict will continue; seven billion people cannot possibly all see things the same way.

Now, if you were to turn the magnifying glass toward your own life and tell the truth: How much of your attention have you invested in the battle to lose weight, stop smoking, or conquer excessive drinking, gambling, sex, or drugs? And how much energy have you given to the battle with your partner, mother, father, son, or daughter? Can you honestly say that fighting to change things has actually changed anything? I'm talking here about real change: the kind of change that puts an end to your suffering, once and for all.

As long as you derive your identity from the world of physical and psychological form, you will attempt to alleviate your suffering by manipulating these forms to suit your agenda for a better life. The unawakened mind will invent a myriad of ways to convince yourself and other people to agree with who you think you are and with what you think you need and want. You may believe that if only you could get rid of your negative thinking, if only you could get more love, if only they would stop speaking to you in that way, if only they would stop being so miserable or angry or busy or sick, then everything would be alright; you'd be happy, fulfilled, and complete. You may think that if you could stop what is happening and make it conform to what you *want* to be happening, then life would be perfect.

You may spend a lifetime—or even lifetimes—looking for what you think is missing, all the time missing what's already right *here* inside you. You may look for romantic relationship to give you love, for success to give you recognition, for money to give you richness, for knowledge to give you power, or for a guru or a deity or God to give you peace. This effort to find a material remedy to what is essentially a spiritual sickness is bound to fail. You may find the relationship, success, money, knowledge, or guru you were looking for, and for a short while there is a sense of fulfillment because you have stopped seeking and in this stopping you feel complete. Inevitably, however, after the honeymoon period, this feeling does not last, because what you think you have found is not real. The true love that you long for is not a thing that another person can give. True recognition is not something that depends on what you do or what you have. True richness is not something found in bricks, gold, or numbers on a piece of paper. True power is not an accolade bestowed upon you when you've learned the spiritual sutras or received your doctorate in theology, psychology, or astrophysics. And true peace cannot be given by anyone, not even by "God Almighty," "the supreme being," or any other image of a higher power.

True love, recognition, richness, power, and peace are invisible, and you cannot find the invisible in the visible. As soon as the temporary relief of satisfying your idea of completeness passes, the urge to seek more of that which you think will give you what you want returns. The seeking mechanism is a continuous movement from perceived lack to perceived fulfillment to disillusionment to longing for fulfillment to looking for something that will satisfy this longing. This sequence takes place in the imagination: it's a horizontal movement of the mind (moving backward and forward from the past to the future), a kind of "mental masturbation" that becomes an addiction. It is this addiction that drives most of humanity's behavior.

To end this addiction is revolutionary. This ending has the power to bring down the entire edifice of your inner and outer world. The decision to stop investing a sense of personal ownership in the movement of the mind, and stop believing that your seeking has any basis in reality, is a radical step toward real change. In this decision, you are offered the opportunity to stop getting lost in the momentum of seeking and to turn your attention to what is truly there, whether seeking happens or not. It's as if the seeking mechanism turns in on itself and seeks that which is within the seeker. This total turnaround in the focus of your attention has the capacity to cut the root of suffering. It's a 360-degree revolution in consciousness that changes everything from the inside out. This inner revolution is the death of all stagnant stories and the birth of something radically vibrant. It's the discovery of who you really are, and the start of a whole new relationship to life.

HEALING THE PRIMAL WOUND

Personal evolution begins when the desire to be free of the tyranny of ego is greater than the need for psychological safety. This is no easy feat, since the egoic need for psychological safety has a tight grip. Real transformation is not something you can just decide to do or make happen because you think it will make you a better person, or make you more spiritual and therefore immune to pain. Rather, it's a tipping point that surfaces in our innermost being when suffering becomes simply too much to bear.

When I refer to suffering, I'm speaking of *psychological* suffering, not of the suffering of the body when it experiences physical pain, nor the atrocities and tragedies that make up the suffering of the world. It's the inevitable mental and emotional *story* of suffering that wraps itself around the naked experience of physical pain or human atrocity. Psychological suffering happens when you tell yourself some kind of story of lack. Perhaps an illness, accident, or disability arrives unbidden into your life, and you tell yourself you're not strong enough. Perhaps your relationship falls apart or your parents don't give you the love you need, and you tell yourself you're not lovable enough, Perhaps you fail to achieve the material or social success you dream of, and you tell yourself you're not special enough. Perhaps life smashes your hopes and brings you to your knees, and you tell yourself you're not worthy enough.

At the core of each of these stories of lack is a sense of incompleteness, a belief that you are separate from the wholeness and goodness of life. This belief can be buried so deeply that you may have no idea that it's driving your perception and experience of life. Instead of looking within you, you will be pulled this way and that way by the vicissitudes of life's display, and you will end up very far away from the wholeness that you already are and always have been.

At some point your life may be rocked by some kind of shock or loss—or the faint rumblings of an unspoken unfulfill-ment can simply no longer be ignored. In these moments, certain layers of protection are peeled back to reveal the wound of separation. This wound has both a personal and a universal dimension. The personal dimension is your story. It's the particular storm that has blown through your life and bent you into a unique shape. The universal dimension is the "original sin" of forgetfulness. It's not a sin in the religious sense of having transgressed God, or even in the moral sense of having done something wrong in the eyes of society; rather, it's a "missing of the mark" by forgetting our true nature as inseparable from life and God. It's the core wound of separation created when consciousness gets lost in the identification with form. It's like a black hole, or a nonlocalized yet very specific energetic experience of "aloneness" that pulls us into the terror of annihilation. It's as if we disappear in the vastness of the universe. Whatever our personal stories are, this black hole is deep inside each of us. It's our common human heritage.

Investigating the validity of this existential terror is the doorway to liberation. But we can't get there unless we're willing to face our personal wounding along the way. Unfortunately, this is something we tend to avoid at all costs. The journey of facing our personal wounds is like peeling layers of an onion; it takes courage and tender honesty to keep diving in. Most of us would rather turn away. Facing darkness and pain is almost certainly at the bottom of our wish list!

Many of us in the Western world are privileged enough not to have the horror of starvation, torture, mutilation, or war knocking on our door. However, if we look a little deeper inside ourselves we'll see that most of us have been subject to (at least to some degree) the emotional trauma that comes with our modern culture's legacy of broken families, childhood neglect and abuse, and school bullying.

Even if you remember your early life as safe, with loving parents and all your material needs provided for, and no major incident that created obvious trauma, there's still likely to be some degree of dysfunction. Perhaps your father was frequently away working long hours to make sure the family's future was secure, or your mother was distracted by having to juggle home and career. Maybe your brother or sister got more attention than you did, or there was a family secret that was never spoken about. Even in the wealthiest, most successful and stable families, there is a hidden dynamic that solidifies a sense of separation. Add to this a prevalence of violence and poverty, drug addiction and alcoholism, unemployment and work dissatisfaction, stress, divorce, loneliness, and lack of community, and it's almost impossible to deny that suffering has been experienced. Yet most of us spend a lifetime—or many lifetimes—running away from what hurts. Our whole conditioning, our parents, our society, and our culture support us in doing anything and everything to avoid or numb out the pain in our hearts and in our souls. We would rather turn to intoxicants, painkillers, or sedatives than face the wound. And if these avoidance strategies seem too extreme, then food, entertainment, texting, and Internet surfing can become acceptable substitutes. If we're lucky, these strategies are a temporary measure, like a Band-Aid. If we're even luckier, they'll stop working altogether and the wound will be exposed. Once that occurs, the search for wholeness can become more conscious.

Today, unlike in our parents' and grandparents' generations, all kinds of psychological methods, therapies, healing modalities, and self-help tools are available. Many of us turn to these in an attempt to heal our nagging sense of incompleteness. While this is a valiant and worthwhile refocusing of our attention, it can be a tricky situation, because once personal wounding is revealed, the attempt to heal it is likely to be unconsciously driven by the desire to get rid of it. This is not a surprise, as this "aversion to pain" mechanism is the driving force behind almost everything we do. It's part of humanity's primal survival instinct. We are compelled to become more lovable, loving, empowered, successful, or more abundant because we believe that if we are perfect or good enough then we will attract only positive experiences and create the exact lives we want. In other words, we attempt to control our life in order to avoid pain. Unless we make the choice to take a different route than this, we will not be free to evolve beyond this primitive mechanism.

Even the spiritual search can become a "bypass method," or a way of avoiding unresolved emotional issues. When all other methods fail to protect us from pain, spirituality offers the salve of transcendence. Some part of you is likely to be greatly relieved to hear that awakening or enlightenment brings an end to suffering. However, when this belief is held onto without honest examination as to its validity, it's nothing more than a convenient avoidance of unwanted emotions—yet another safety strategy employed by the ego. The fantasy of a pain-free life is a tenacious one and the mind makes up many stories about what awakening or enlightenment looks like. None of these are true. The reality is that by sitting inside the brokenness of your personal story and surrendering to the futility of searching for a pain-free life, you can discover the shimmering radiance that remains unbroken and unblemished in it all. When suffering or pain is fully met in the open space of unconditional acceptance, you are offered the possibility of discovering who you are beneath it. It ends the story of wounding once and for all, and heals the "original sin" of forgetfulness.

TELLING THE TRUTH

The more spiritual you think you are, the more ruthlessly honest you need to be. This includes the story of your life and all the raw feelings and turbulent or confusing emotions contained within it. There's a tendency in some spiritual seekers to deny their story. While believing that your story is who you really are is insanity, denying your story is ludicrous. Your story is an inevitable part of how you experience life today, a part of your body-mind vehicle and its expression. The willingness to embrace personal truth in the search for absolute truth is a necessary component of the authentic embodiment of awakened consciousness. This doesn't mean you should blame yourself or your family. Nor does it mean blaming life or God for what appears to hurt. It does mean, however, fully acknowledging and meeting that which hurts. Unfortunately, many people who have glimpsed the unattainability of unconditioned awareness continue to resist this meeting place, as if the messiness of personal truth somehow tarnishes the pristine clarity of absolute truth. And yet, the luminous truth of awakeness cannot be fully integrated into human life if the layers of personal truth are not fully welcomed in all their horror and agony. At some point, the willingness to stop running away from what hurts and to face whatever is appearing in life becomes of the utmost priority. Perhaps this moment has already appeared for you, and reading these words simply strengthens your commitment to this path. Or if that commitment has not yet come, maybe something in you knows it is unavoidable.

The commitment to telling the truth is like a missile that seeks out everything that has been hiding in the shadows; but unlike a missile, it doesn't destroy. It does something far more powerful: it transmutes. The sincere search for truth—a search that includes everything in its path and leaves nothing in its slipstream—lights a fire that calls everything home to its true nature. It's only in the glaring spotlight of radiant awareness that the layers of hurt can be purified. And in this fire of truth, they are given the opportunity to return to their original state as love—innocent and free.

Often it is difficult to see, let alone to welcome, that which has hardened into a story of "me." There's a certain comfort, or at least a familiarity, to the habitual constructs, concepts, and ideas that define who you think you are. But who you think you are is not who you really are. You are so much deeper than any story of who you are. You are so much more luminous than the scaffolding erected to uphold a sense of "me."

This scaffolding is nothing more than a defense structure or set of conditioned responses based on the psychological movement toward what you like (because it makes you feel safe, loved, worthy, and so on) and away from what you dislike (because it makes you feel unsafe, unloved, unworthy, and so on). Every time there is a psychological movement, there is a labeling of the experience as right or wrong, good or bad, perfect or imperfect, and so on. This habit of dividing every experience reflects a basic nonacceptance of things as they are, and when this is expressed it becomes a grievance. Resentment, blame, anger, disappointment, regret, self-pity, self-righteousness, and superiority are all grievances. Every grievance is an energetic contraction that perpetuates the story of who you think you are.

Beneath all the opinions, arguments, and judgments, there's a wide-open space within which all division dissolves. The scaffolding of who you think you are appears to have a lot of substance or density to it, but in fact it is quite flimsy because it's an illusion. If, for a moment, you stop giving your attention to the upholding of the scaffolding by constantly categorizing, labeling, and dividing your experience, and instead turn inward to the investigation of what is within each contraction as it appears, there is the possibility of discovering your true nature.

FALLING INTO THE ABYSS OF BEING

Turning inward is often scary, because it brings up the terror of death. It brings you face to face with the abyss that lies beneath the scaffolding. The scaffolding is everything that is familiar— your beliefs, your habitual ways of seeing and experiencing life, and all the thoughts and emotions that create a sense of identity. The abyss is what you cannot possibly know, because it's totally unknowable by the egoic mind. By acknowledging that your mind does not actually know the truth of who you are, who you are can be revealed.

In spiritual circles, the question "Who am I?" is central to the inquiry into the true nature of self. However, this inquiry is often hijacked by the ego in an attempt to avoid facing the terror of death. Instead, the ego may come up with definitions of who you are: "I am oneness," "I am divine," "I am everything," or even "I am nothing." But who you really are is not another more spiritual, perfect, or divine form of scaffolding. Who you really are has no definition: it is an indescribable, unspeakable depth of being.

The true purpose of the question "Who am I?" is to serve as a pointer to diving into the unknownness of this unbounded moment. It's a question without an answer, a koan, a signpost to the edge of mind, where you are invited to take a leap. Here you have a choice: to go running back to the relative safety of the story of "me" or to let go into the unknown. If you let go, you open up to the possibility of total annihilation of the scaffolding that defends all your ideas and concepts about who you think you are. It's a free fall into the abyss of being that literally stops the mind. In this momentary stopping, there is a shift in consciousness to a deeper dimension of being, a coming home to your true nature. Coming home is what each of us yearns for. It's the ultimate fulfillment, a sense of completeness, and a feeling of being totally at one with yourself and with life.

Any addictive behavior, whether it be compulsive smoking, the satisfaction of sexual impulses, getting high on recreational drugs, eating for comfort, or shopping therapy, is driven by a hardwired desire to lose ourselves in the primordial oneness of the womb. Most people understand intuitively what it means to yearn for the undifferentiated consciousness before we are born. All addictions are an unconscious yearning for this. It's our deepest longing for absolute union, an ancient pull toward innocent oblivion. It's the innate memory of that which exists prior to form: pure being.

But when this desire is unconscious—in other words, when it is owned by the ego—we look in a direction that can never bring fulfillment. It's like looking at the waves and trying to catch hold of one that takes your fancy: as soon as you attempt to possess it, it slips through your fingers and you go on searching for another wave again and again. The same is true with the search to fulfill your deepest longing, because this longing is never-ending. Anything you imagine that might bring you true happiness and lasting peace is simply that: an imagination, an idea, a hope.

If you are lucky enough to see the elusive nature of this "wave chasing," the search can then be redirected to a more conscious desire for fulfillment. What often follows is an attempt to develop positive qualities that enhance a sense of emotional and spiritual well-being. In our modern-day culture of self-empowerment, there are many tools and techniques for cultivating gratitude, forgiveness, acceptance, letting go, loving kindness, and the like. While all of these are wonderful steps toward growing beyond self-limiting beliefs, there's a tendency to get stuck in a "spiritual shopping" syndrome in the attempt to cultivate fulfillment. But true fulfillment is not an accumulation of spiritual qualities; rather, it is an emptying of the "spiritual shopping basket." It's a ruthlessly honest letting go of all ideas that uphold a sense of identity. This is not as easy as you'd think, especially if you consider yourself to be spiritual. This "emptying" brings you face to face with everything you have been conditioned to believe about yourself.

Coming home to true oneness is an unknown dimension of being; a dimension so immensely open that no self can be found in it. It is a death, not a gain. The invitation to finally discover what you have been searching for requires the willingness to fall off the edge of the mind and into the unknown vista of unboundedness. It's a moment-to-moment "dying into emptiness," a vertical deep dive. Along the way, there is the high likelihood of an encounter with every energetic contraction that upholds the scaffolding of self-identity. When fully met, these contractions are liberated. When welcomed into the clear light of awareness, every phenomenal display, feeling, thought, and sensation dies into nothingness. It returns to source. It is the ungraspable openness of this forever-unfolding moment that we both fear and long for. We fear it because it is unimaginable; it is unknowable to the mind. We long for it because somewhere in our hearts, we know it is inseparable from our innermost being.

The attempt to feel safe by clinging to a sense of self derived from a set of thoughts, ideas, and beliefs is a complete illusion. There is, in fact, no knownness. Every moment is unknown as it unfolds before you. Every moment is fresh and carries the potential for both discomfort and wonderment. Every moment is born anew, arising out of the unconditioned field of the absolute and expressing itself through the relativity of the phenomenal experience. No moment can ever be repeated. The attempt to feel safe in order to avoid any potential discomfort is a "numbing out" that only serves to separate you from your aliveness and the aliveness inherent in all forms. It is this that creates the resistance and the discomfort, not the content of the moment itself. When you realize that *nothing* is known and *everything* is unknown, then you can find deep comfort in this realization. And what was dead, shallow, and stagnant becomes alive, deep, and vibrant.

The invitation is right here, in *this* very moment, for you to stop and to recognize that you are already home. In this stopping, and in this moment, you can start truly living.

THE MYTH OF ENLIGHTENMENT

There's something that often stands in the way of falling into the abyss of being and truly living the unbounded aliveness of awakeness: the mind-created ideas of what spiritual liberation looks like. We could call this the "myth of enlightenment." It's a myth because it is not real, and also because it's a delusion that many spiritual seekers encounter.

In this enduring and alluring myth, the enlightened one lives a perfect life in which no pain is experienced. Always calm, loving, and selfless, even in the midst of challenging circumstances, they never experience irritation, sadness, frustration, or anger. This special person exists in a special world beyond the messiness of human feelings. Floating about on a bubble of bliss without any personal or worldly desires, the enlightened one could be said to have magical powers that elevate them above mere mortal status.

It's certainly an immature picture of enlightenment, but honest investigation is likely to reveal that this (or perhaps a slightly more sophisticated version of it) is very common. It's like the proverbial carrot that is dangled on the end of a stick, keeping the donkey plodding along the path without ever attaining its much-desired reward. Like the donkey, many spiritual seekers, despite their deep desire for awakening and their commitment to the spiritual path, never reach the promised land of enlightenment. The mind creates all sorts of complex reasons as to why the carrot is unattainable. But enlightenment doesn't look the way we think it does—or the way we want it to.

Once the defensive structures that create the scaffolding that upholds the sense of "me" inevitably come tumbling down, and the luminous truth of you has been recognized, it's also inevitable that certain mental, emotional, and karmic tendencies continue to express themselves. After enlightenment there is still a human being with flaws, because form is always tainted in some way. The personality-vehicle is bent into and out of shape by the particular storm that blows through your life: this is your personal story. It may have been a gentle breeze, or it may have been a tornado; either way, it has created a unique appearance as you. Depending on the environment, circumstances, and the specifics of unconscious conditioning, the personality may exhibit all kinds of preferences, predispositions, and apparent imperfections.

But it is not the individual "person" that *becomes* enlightened. Rather, the empty radiance of your true nature as formlessness is simply revealed. This is universal because this empty radiance is at the core of all that exists. From the perspective of this absolute reality, everything is perfect as it is, including powerful or dark emotions, addictions, and even resistance. The absolute is untainted by any phenomenal display. The inherent awakeness of your true nature is not dependent on any particular phenomenon. This is where the myth of enlightenment gets in the way.

One of the most common errors on the spiritual path is the tendency to believe that enlightenment will happen to "you." When the bliss of pure being has actually been tasted, the tendency is to want to hide within the pain-free zone of the absolute and deny the human experience. Before enlightenment, this leads to the "donkey and the carrot" syndrome. After enlightenment, this leads to the playing out of the shadow, or the unconscious spilling out of suppressed energies.

If awakeness is to be a living truth, the demand is for a deeper vigilance. This is especially important in the surprise that comes when you see that while the scaffolding that upholds a false sense of "me" comes tumbling down, the imperfect personality continues to function even after awakening. It's at this stage that a real inner transformation can happen. However, if there is a refusal to see that the personality is still functioning, then this transformation cannot even begin.

If you are authentically committed to opening to the whole of you, even though it may hurt your pride, make you cringe in disgust, or bring you to your knees in shame, then the empty radiance at the core of all that you perceive, think, and feel will pour into you unimpeded. As this formless unconditioned awakeness flows through you and into your life, a natural state of beingness reveals itself as causeless joy and love. It's a joy and a love without object or subject and therefore unconstrained by any form, whether that form be an emotion, a feeling, or a thought.

This "flowing into" is an ongoing journey of the continual willingness to meet all gross and subtle contractions in the light of awareness. When fully allowed in each new moment and circumstance, it becomes a purifying process that dissolves the residue of negative, pessimistic, dark feelings, as well as the addictive movements of the mind. The purification of the mind-body vehicle is like polishing the sides of a diamond: as the dusty layers of habitual tendencies are lifted, the light of unconditioned awakeness emanates and radiates through you as you. This is when the outer form of personality bows down in service to innermost being, and there is an alignment of truth as living reality.

The grace of it all is that even though there's undoubtedly a unique individual expression, the subjective experience of personality is permeable and transparent. There's a sweet nakedness because there's nothing to cling to, nothing to uphold, nothing to hide from, and nothing to run away from. Every construct previously created as a defense system is seen as a futile attempt to protect a false idea of self, and so it is all willingly surrendered into the abyss of open unknownness. Everything simply and gracefully flows through, even the most painful of experiences, because everything *is* you. How can you deny the truth of this when you know yourself to be inseparable from existence itself? In whatever form, whether as a thought, emotion, or circumstance, that which appears is irrevocably here and it can be met all the way. In the nakedness of this meeting, the heart is broken open, and then whatever experience, however intense, is gone; there is nothing to stick to. When emptiness is realized as your truest nature, then all is dissolved and resolved in this.

INTEGRATING THE SHADOW AND ALLOWING SUPPORT

The striving for spiritual attainment while excluding the personal dimension of life is a big error. Ignoring unresolved psychological contractions is a danger that is frequently overlooked in the process of awakening. Of course, for some, awakening happens spontaneously even when psychological contractions have not been faced, but it doesn't make your problems go away! Your life mostly continues along the same groove, and this is fine if there is a deep acceptance of that fact and you don't expect any particular expression of your life to change. What happens all too commonly, however, is that there's a denial that there are any remaining inner blockages to attend to.

When we disown the parts of ourselves that we believe to be unacceptable or unenlightened, they get thrown into a metaphorical shadow-bag. When these unconscious inner forces remain unacknowledged or unexamined, they inevitably take possession of the pristine peace of the unconditioned awake state and play havoc with our internal and external environment. These unconscious inner forces can become troublesome because they've been pushed away for so long. Eventually, they will reveal themselves in distorted and catastrophic ways. Mental and emotional breakdowns are a symptom of this, as are power struggles, inappropriate and even abusive sexual relationships, and hidden greed or corruption.

If there has not been an honest opening to all psychological contractions, then inner division will continue, even if you are awakened. This is especially so in the initial stage of awakening, when the ego easily takes ownership and obscures any suppressed energies. If this subtle identification with the awakened state remains hidden, the full integration of awakening into ordinary life, as it descends from mind to heart to body, is hindered. Even Buddha had to sit under the Bodhi Tree, immovable, while Mara, the Lord of Darkness, tempted him with desires and tormented him with fears, before enlightenment became his living reality. Jesus had to meet his demons in the desert before he could abide permanently in the light of true spiritual awakening.

The embodiment of awakeness requires a healing of inner division. This is more likely to happen if body-mind contractions are fully met and dissolved. Here, psychological work can be a great support. Awakening is not about self-improvement; it's about the intelligent investigation of hidden inner dynamics that may otherwise remain inaccessible. While awakening *can* happen in any moment, it doesn't necessarily unstick things in the human realm or heal any woundedness that may be held within the subconscious.

There is a need for the integration of the shadow, especially in the Western psyche. Where there is a pervading culture of dysfunction and abuse that solidifies the belief in the wounded self and stories of victimhood, there is still a constructive role for therapy that can facilitate the meeting of painful feelings that are habitually avoided. Anxiety, depression, traumas, and addictions can all be invited into the meeting place of psychology and nondual spirituality. Here, there is a gentle allowing of all energies while pointing to the unconditioned space of awareness throughout it all. When trauma or emotional suppression run deep, energetic blockages can often more easily be released through bodywork within the same context of awareness. In the vessel of love, without expectation of any particular outcome, there is a natural unfoldment and stabilization of awakened consciousness.

Many people hope that awakening will make all the pain disappear. But the wisdom and humility to allow support where it is needed, even after awakening, is a great support in itself. It is inevitable that the personality and sense of self reappear within awakened consciousness, and there may be ensuing disappointment or confusion, especially if there is unresolved trauma or addictive patterns and no previous inner work has been done. Whether support comes in the form of therapy, the continuation of meditative practice, the reflection of unconditioned awareness from a spiritual teacher, or an openhearted conversation with a friend, the willingness to meet all that continues to reveal itself with tenderness is what matters.

The invitation here is for you to do what needs to be done, without agenda. Very often we barter with life or with God, thinking that if we roll up our sleeves and dig into the dirt, we are guaranteed permanent enlightenment. But the embodiment of awakening is not a bartering system, because awakeness has no "self" invested in it. The invitation is for you to allow support where necessary, to be honest with yourself, to be willing to be humble and tender, and to support awakeness as it seeks to become embodied through you, *as* you.

DOES THE EGO DIE?

Another tenacious concept that perpetuates the myth of enlightenment and creates much confusion in the spiritual seeker is the belief that the ego dies, and with it all personal history is erased. In this myth, the "enlightened one" supposedly has no sense of self and no story, and therefore he or she is expected to never talk about themselves, to never use the word "I" or "me," and to never refer to "my life." The "enlightened one" has supposedly seen that the body and the world are an illusion, and therefore is totally unconcerned with physical well-being or worldly affairs. This image of enlightenment is a fantasy upheld by millennia of religious dogma and patriarchal spiritual traditions. It also taps into our childlike need to enter the kingdom of heaven or nirvana, where bad things never happen and we are rewarded with endless peace.

The stark reality is that awakening is not a death of the ego. As long as you're alive as form, the ego cannot die. Ego, as a primary sense of "I-ness," must exist, otherwise you'd be unable to discern inside from outside. It's very likely that, without an ego, the voices in your head would be undifferentiated from my voice, from someone else's voice, or from the voice of God, and you would be in a state of psychosis. You might even be a blubbery mess, unable to function in three-dimensional reality. If you've ever taken too many psychedelics, you'll know how disorientating and even terrifying this can be!

As long as we operate within relative reality, the relative function of ego must continue to operate. A sense of self as a separate entity is absolutely necessary for both physical and psychological survival as form. Death of ego only happens when form dies. Luckily, as long as there is a functioning neurophysiology, there is a sense of self. It is this sense of "I" that increasingly develops as we emerge from the womb and gives us the capacity for self-reflection or self-awareness. It's actually the seed of awakening, because without it we would not be able to become conscious of consciousness.

Awakening is also not a transcendence of ego. Transcendence of ego certainly can happen in a variety of circumstances, such as when you experience a mystical state or a state of expanded consciousness such as in deep meditation (*samadhi*), long-distance running, or giving birth. It also happens if you have an out-of-body experience or near-death experience. The initial experience of awakening can also be an intensely transcendent experience. But if you continue to identify with this transcendent state, you are likely to develop a "spiritual ego." There is no transformation or evolution of consciousness in the identification with this state, because when the inevitable return of old egoic patterns and personality traits appear there is a tendency to deny that any of this belongs to you.

In true awakening, there is neither a death nor a transcendence of ego. Instead, the location of self is released from its entanglement with the unconscious ego (in other words, the conglomeration of conditioned mental, emotional, and physical responses). Liberated from the prison of egoic identification, the sense of "I-ness" becomes nonlocalized and unattached. Having recognized awakeness as the inherent nature of all that is (including the self), the self becomes an "awake I," undefined and unrestrained by relative reality.

Another way of saying this is that the self experiences itself as inseparable from the totality of existence. While certain survival-based impulses continue (protecting the body from danger, the impulse to eat when hungry, drink when thirsty, or rest when tired, and so on), these now happen without interference. They simply happen as life's natural and intelligent movement toward what needs attention while form is alive. The "awake I" is therefore free to respond intelligently and creatively to the moment, and this gives you access to a power that is at one with life itself.

So what happens to the ego in all this? From one perspective, nothing changes. The ego continues to operate, to keep form alive. From another perspective, everything changes. In the process of liberation, the once unconscious ego transmutes to an evolved or "aware ego" and gives itself in service to the "awake I." In other words, the ego stops being the master and bows down to awakeness.

So, yes, in awakening there is a death. There is a death of the self-identity that is wrapped around ego. But there is also a birth of a whole, integrated human being that includes both the surface sense of self as a separate entity (the self that is born and then dies) *and* the deeper layer of undifferentiated beingness (the self that was never born and can never die).

Awakeness embraces the paradox of self and no-self. There is no conflict in this apparent duality. While the mind finds this intolerable, the heart abides in unfathomable acceptance. When the silent mystery of spacious acceptance becomes over-ridingly preferable to the habitual struggle of making sense of it all, the search for a mythical state of enlightenment comes to an end. However, the ever-unfolding deepening into authentic awakening never stops.

CHAPTER 4

Deepening Into Being

THE END OF SEEKING

Once awakeness has been recognized, it's easy to fall back into complacency and laziness. We may think, if the light has been turned on, there is nothing more to do. But authentic awakening is radical. It is not something that we do for 20 minutes twice a day and then tick off our "to do" list—it's a 24-hour-a-day, 365-days-a-year job that calls us to be ruthlessly honest. You either meet life consciously or you get lost in the dream. There's no halfway. You can't be semi-conscious. You can't meet life consciously only when it feels good or you get things to go your way, but then get lost in the story when it all goes wrong or it hurts. What you *can* do is become aware of what is still unconscious in you. This resolve to be vigilant is the fertilizer for the deeper awakening required if there is to be a real transformation in your inner and outer world.

Whether you have temporarily glimpsed an awakened state that has vanished, or the light of awakening has revealed itself as the background of your life, or even if you have not yet glimpsed awakening but something inexorably draws you toward it, there is very possibly something in these words that will fan the flame of truth so that it becomes a furnace of radical awakeness within you. When this furnace has consumed all false notions of what an awakened life should look like, the incessant search for anything other than this ever-unfolding moment comes to an end. And what remains is an unending river of grace, both ineffably divine and utterly ordinary.

The discovery that allows you to finally rest in this river of grace does not require your past to be healed of what was broken nor for your future to be more wonderful than what is happening now. The recognition of awakeness as the inherent nature of all things, including oneself, puts an end to the endless search for a better self or a better life. It's the end of seeking and the beginning of the possibility of true healing.

This opportunity for healing comes when there is a conscious willingness to open to the totality of you. This willingness is an all or nothing affair. For true healing to take place, you can't just open to the bits you like and circumvent the rest. You have to embrace the whole lot, the light and the dark, the enlightened and the unenlightened, the heavenly and the hellish. This is a kind of responsibility in which the "awake I" chooses to give itself in service to awakeness itself. This isn't about achieving a state of perfection. It's about welcoming the light of awakeness into everyday life.

When awakening is embodied, there is an abiding recognition that nothing can touch, taint, or harm the beingness of which you are the living expression. While the ripples of your story continue to reverberate through your body-mind experience, and when discomfort, irritation, anger, or anything else arises, you will not cling to the idea that you need more healing or therapy to get rid of this apparently unenlightened energy. Instead you will rest in the truth of your unadulterated nature and simply meet the energy with tender curiosity.

It's the capacity to be fully with what is that creates healing or wholeness. In this deep acceptance, you see that light is the nature of darkness. Awakeness does not deny the past, the history of your life, the memories, the disappointments, the heartbreaks, the regrets, and even what appear as past-life experiences. All these can be embraced in present-moment awareness so that past and future are seen to occur in the now, which is an ever-unfolding eternal moment. Your woundedness is, in fact, not what happened to you in the past, but rather your inability to stay present and open in the face of what happened. In present-moment awareness you can meet the hurt of this disconnect. And in this there is a reconnection and a healing.

It's a fact that life will always touch you, bump into you, cut you, and even scar you in some way. But who you really are remains untouched and unscathed throughout it all. Opening up to this paradox of human existence means you become more vast than who you think you are. In this vastness, you live from the space and the silence within you. When you see that everything that happens in your inner and outer world is actually appearing within this space and silence, then there is nothing more to do in order to awaken, nothing more to achieve or attain. The search for enlightenment has ended.

LIVING AS SILENCE

We mostly think of silence as the opposite of noise, as something we can find by getting away from our everyday lives, or something we can create by switching off the phone, lighting a few candles, and relaxing on the couch. But silence is not an object or a commodity. It can neither be found nor created in the horizontal dimension of egoic consciousness.

Silence is ever-present in everything. It exists prior to all form. It is the groundless ground of being. You don't have to go anywhere or do anything to find it, because it's actually who you are. Silence is the nature of your innermost being, and when you wake up out of the dream of mistaken identity, you discover that you, too, are in fact inseparable from this silence.

Silence is what is here when you stop giving your attention to the movement of the mind and stop following the thoughts "I need to find time for silence," "I have to get away from all this business to get some peace," or "If only I could stop the thoughts in my head." In seeing the illusory nature of this kind of thinking and the futility of all running away or running toward, you come to a full stop, and what is revealed in this stopping is the ever-present silence of pure being. This full stop is not a head-on collision with something hard and finite. Instead, it is open-ended: silence has no boundary, no landing place, no center, no location, and no reference point for where it begins or ends. You find yourself in a new dimension of seeing in which awareness is recognized as the only fact of reality. When this awareness falls back into itself and becomes rooted in itself, an unlimited unconditional silence is revealed at the core of everything experienced, whether it be the whisper of the wind or the thunder of a mega-ton truck on the highway.

The majority of people, in the unilluminated state of consciousness, are so identified with the thoughts in their heads that they are totally unaware of the silence within. They mistakenly believe that everything has to be quiet in order for silence to be heard. But silence is inclusive: the chirp of the bird at your window, the song on the radio, the cry of the baby, the lapping of the waves on the shore, the piercing scream of a motorbike engine, all these sounds arise out of silence and return to silence. In order to recognize this silence, there needs to be a willingness to let go of all labels and concepts of who you think you are, as well as to relinquish all labels and concepts around how you see life. In other words, you need to stop clutching at the thoughts in your head as if they were a life raft and let go into the unknown. Most people, however, are unwilling to face the terror of death, both psychological death and physical death, so they're actually afraid of silence.

In order to hear silence, you need to listen with the emptiness of beingness. This requires that you open to the deeper, ungraspable dimension within yourself and the world. Of course this openness makes you feel vulnerable because it dissolves the mind-created boundary between "me" and "you" and "me" and "the world." The tendency is to retract from it, but the invitation of silence is to fall off the edge of this boundary. You need to be willing to drown in that which is unfettered by your fear, and give yourself totally to the freedom of the unknown. At first, this unknownness is something you can dip your toe into, but there comes a time on the journey of inner transformation when you are called to dive into it completely. You cannot be partly free, freedom is total.

In the full light of awakening, silence becomes the song of your life. It is the constant backdrop to the scenes acted upon it. Silent awareness is the primary experience out of which everything—thought, feeling, sensation, image, object—arises as a secondary experience. When there is no attempt to change, manipulate, gloss over, or turn the dial up or down on this secondary manifestation, there is choiceless awareness. This is a full allowing of everything into the field of awareness. Nothing is excluded and yet everything is seen to be ever-changing and therefore impermanent. Emptiness is full, and fullness is empty.

When silence fully reveals itself as the ground of being, and when you are fully open to this inner dimension of beingness, then the busyness of life doesn't make an iota of difference in the primordial state of things. Whether you're sitting still with no noise in the vicinity, or you're in the midst of a bustling marketplace, who you really are is untouched by any of it. Both action and nonaction are experienced as an extension of silence.

Now you live *in* silence, *from* silence … and *as* silence.

IS MEDITATION NECESSARY?

Many people on the spiritual path ask, "Is meditation necessary for silence to be recognized?" This is a question that requires a delicate answer, because it really depends on where you are on your path. The majority of humanity is unaware that thinking comes and goes within the bigger context of space, and so they have no spaciousness in their consciousness. Meditation, whether it be Transcendental Meditation, Vipassana, Zen, or any other kind of meditation practice, brings attention to the witnessing aspect of self and helps to create a space between the witness and that which is being witnessed. In other words, it dissolves identification with thinking. This is tremendously useful for the cultivation of an unconditioned spaciousness. For many people, this is a great relief from being totally caught up in the noisiness of incessant thinking, and it brings a sense of peacefulness.

But meditation itself is not freedom. There is no guarantee that meditation practice will lead to awakening. On the contrary, for many seekers the practice of meditation can become a blind spot on the journey toward a deeper dimension of inner beingness. It sometimes can become a hindrance to the more profound openness required for true awakening. The most sublime or transcendent states of sheer silence can be reached in meditation, and still nothing will change in everyday life because there is a subtle hankering after these states (and, like all states, these come and go). This is not freedom. Another common blind spot happens when there's an identification with being a "meditator." A subtle arrogance can then arise from two common misconceptions: the belief in the concept of *progress* as a spiritual seeker, and the belief that *doing something* can make awakening happen.

In true awakening, silence reveals itself without a doubt as the true nature of unbounded mind and heart. Most often, if meditation has been a practice, once this awakening happens the practice simply falls away. It is an unnecessary prop. Sometimes awakening can happen even when there has been no experience of meditation practice at all. The danger here is that this awakening isn't easily stabilized and as any energetic contractions are encountered, the light of this awakened consciousness can get dimmer. In this case, the "practice of silence" can serve to deepen and restabilize the realization of emptiness.

But when the "practice" of anything is seen to be a pointless mind-created structure, the real meaning of meditation can reveal itself. Meditation is ultimately neither a technique nor a method. It is, in fact, a state of being. It's the moment-to-moment awareness of what is. It's as simple as that. Meditation doesn't require a special environment or a specific posture. It's not located in space or time. It is *this* moment pointing you back home over and over again. It's the timelessness of the present and it doesn't require you to go anywhere or do anything.

True meditation is waking up out of the nightmare of thought-generated reality and entering the kingdom of heaven. If you are always willing to devote yourself to *this* moment, you will discover the peace that is always here.

DEVOTION TO THIS MOMENT

This moment is ineffably intimate; it cannot be any other way. This moment is always *here;* it never leaves you, it never abandons you, runs away from you, or hides from you. Wherever you are, this moment is here with you, right up close, always giving itself to you. There are no pretenses, no defenses, no masks. This moment is always *as it is* … raw, naked, shameless … fully itself. This moment gives everything to you. It's the full depth and breadth of every experience, permutation, possibility, and phenomenal display. All this is given unconditionally— the horror, terror, agony, beauty, and ecstasy—it is all *here.*

Take a moment to rest here. Allow yourself to open to *all that is.* Can you get a sense of the incredible tapestry of life? Can you sense the exquisiteness and richness of *this?* Can you see how every wave that appears in the field of your perception is unique, and that there are an infinite number of waves? No two waves are ever the same; each moment is born anew. What endless creativity! This moment is truly in love with you and completely devoted to you. This love is limitless and unbounded; it does not deny you anything. This love is not conditional on whether you give something back or whether you give nothing back. It has nothing to do with whether you love or hate this moment, or whether you are at peace or at war with this moment. It is *here,* come what may, whether you are here or not! Living the truth of awakening can be summed up as the full recognition and acceptance of the fact that this moment is totally here and devoted to you whether you like this moment or not.

Your willingness to get right up close and intimate with this moment is the doorway to authentic liberation, moment by moment. You can be awake to your true nature yet still afraid to be intimate, especially when powerful or dark emotions arise. Usually, it's an intimate relationship that triggers these unwanted energies. Sometimes it's the darkness in the world that is unwanted. Hiding behind an "I'm enlightened, nothing can touch me" attitude is an avoidance of being pierced by the heart of reality. It's a turning away from the full depth and breadth of this moment, a denial of the light offered in the darkest of places.

The mind-shattering magnificence of existence can only be truly revealed to you in the willingness to be open to intimacy and everything that appears in your field of experience in each moment. This includes being open to your fear, resistance, and contraction. It's about being intimate with intimacy itself. There's no "how to" guide for this. It's for *you* to discover for yourself. How can *you* be intimate with the rawness of this moment? It's for *you* to discover that this rawness demands your vulnerability, and to see what lies inside this vulnerability. The question is: Are you willing to be open? Are you willing to even consider that vulnerability is the key to an unending intimacy with life that makes you invulnerable to the inherent changeability of the world of form? Are you willing to be intimate with a life that transcends both birth and death? As Jesus said: "The world is passing away, and also its lusts; but the one who does the will of God lives forever."[2] He was referring to the possibility of discovering your eternal nature when you bring the depth of your presence and the breadth of your openness to this moment.

Beyond any surface resistance, numbing, or contraction, you are *here* totally; it cannot be any other way. The depth of you, the innocence of you, the innermost of you is always here in this moment *as* this moment. And your willingness to accept this at the deepest level of your being has the capacity to turn you inside out so that you become a naked lover of life. This moment is so precious because it is the doorway to everything you have ever longed for. This moment unashamedly offers you the opportunity to finally surrender all the way and enter the full glory of spiritual liberation as a fully authentic human being.

CHAPTER 5

Beyond Awakening, Embracing the World

SPIRITUAL MATURITY AND THE THREE STAGES OF AWAKENING

Perhaps, dear reader, it is now becoming evident that there are many delicate unfoldings on the journey of inner transformation and finding freedom. It's not as black and white as we'd like to believe. You don't just wake up one day and become enlightened. And the world doesn't suddenly become perfect. Maybe you can now see that there is awakening and there is the *maturation* of awakening. It's the maturation part that is so relevant to the complexity of our modern-day culture and psyche. Most often, there is confusion around what this maturation looks like and what it means to actually live an awakened life.

Awakening is the initial recognition of that which is awake in you. It's the moment when you wake up out of the slumber of mistaken identity and open your eyes to the light of your essential nature. The maturation of awakening is like the process of a tiny bud becoming a flower. Only a flower in full bloom can fulfill its divine destiny by revealing the beauty of its true colors and by releasing the intoxication of its fragrance. The flower is neither trying to give anything nor trying to get anything and yet its beauty and fragrance are freely available; it is simply being itself. In full embodiment of awakening, that which moves through you as "your life" will be given in service to the awakeness inherent in all things. Just like the flower, you have no choice; you are simply being yourself. There is no division here; no trying to give anything or get anything. It is the heart of *you* meeting the heart of *what is.*

The outermost expression of this maturation is unique to you. Just as every flower has a unique shape and color, the life of each awakened individual has an utterly unique appearance. For some it is expressed more outwardly; for example, through the inspiration to build an ethical business, the desire to offer a service through work within a community or organization, the impulse to support others on their personal journey (perhaps by being a therapist, life-coach, or a spiritual teacher), or through the expression of creative arts. For others it is more of an inward expression; for example, through a contemplative life of living in a spiritual community, gardening, writing poetry, or simply by being very present while making a cup of tea or walking the dog. Either way, outward or inward, what you *do* is in service to the truth of reality rather than to the egoic need for self-comfort or self-importance. Initially, it is very likely that the pull is further inward into stillness and solitude. But as time progresses, that which moves through you is likely to draw you back into the world, where you can better serve the illumination of all beings.

This maturation process is of particular relevance to today's spiritual seeker living an ordinary life, because it can only take place in the cauldron of everyday human interactions. The messy world of taking care of the body's needs, relationships, raising a family, and working is where the jewel of awakeness is polished. But this is not really news, because ancient spiritual texts, such as those that arose out of the philosophies of yoga, Vedanta, and tantra, also talk about three stages of awakening that point to the same process. Each so-called "stage" offers a useful signpost as to where we might be stuck or deluding ourselves that we have arrived at the holy grail of enlightenment.

The first stage comes with a radical shift in perception: the world of form is seen to be impermanent and therefore without real substance. This razor-sharp cognition of the illusory nature of that which we previously assumed to be solid or stable is a shock to the mind. In a traditional spiritual context, this realization would most often result from rigorous meditative practice. Today, psychedelics, psychological stress, deep grief, loss or pain, or even just being still in the presence of extreme beauty in nature can all be catalysts for shaking us out of the prison of ego's way of seeing things.

Initially, this is experienced as "the high of liberation," a state of bliss, oneness, or intense joy. This may last for just a few minutes, a few days, or even several months. As previously unchallenged assumptions about reality come tumbling down, there is often an accompanying degree of disillusionment. As the world and normal life come back into view, they can appear to be meaningless, and confusion, insecurity, despair, and fear are common responses. While the truth in you rejoices that a deeper reality has been glimpsed, the ego is threatened by this new perspective and scrambles to make sense of it. In the attempt to hold on to an idea of safety, security, or sanity, there is a reidentification with an archaic sense of self, based on solid form.

This split between true seeing and egoic perception perpetuates a discomfort, a sense that things are not quite right. Awakening seems to have happened and yet there is still not an abiding sense of peace. Surely something is missing from the whole picture. What follows is usually an attempt to recapture the high of liberation by looking for the right method, knowledge, or teacher. In this case, the ego is still trying to "do something" to achieve a permanent awakened state.

If this attempt to hold onto awakening is recognized as erroneous, there is likely to be a deeper seeing (traditionally called the second stage). This is a revelation of the luminosity that remains when everything falls apart, an undeniable awareness of enduring emptiness as the ground of reality. Although there is the possibility of deep rest here, there's also a strong tendency to get stuck here. Identification with eternal stillness is very tempting. For where there is no movement, there cannot be any suffering, and this is very appealing to the ego, which wants to avoid meeting pain. An example of this is when someone at one of my retreats dramatically stormed out of a talk because I spoke of the capacity to meet personal suffering, as well as the suffering of the world, as a doorway to the unbounded compassion that comes with authentic awakening. In his eyes, suffering was an absolute illusion and therefore not worthy of inquiry. While not always as extreme as this, this example is a common reaction at this stage.

In some ways, this retreat participant was right: suffering is indeed an illusion at the absolute level. But it's not the whole picture. Fixating on emptiness creates another division. And where there is division, however subtle, there cannot be full awakening. It's a spiritually rigid viewpoint that denies being wholeheartedly touched by life—an avoidance of the blood, sweat, and tears that are an inevitable part of the human experience. It's almost as if there is a fear that being human will get in the way of the ultimate transcendent state. Unfortunately, this stance leads to another veil: spiritual arrogance, superiority, and righteousness.

The wholeness of full awakening is described by what is often called the third and final stage. (Remember, these stages are really just signposts, not necessarily linear stages.) The final stage is the recognition that relative and absolute reality are one. Here, the witness and that which is being witnessed—both the subject and the object—collapse into each other. You are both the emptiness of being and the fullness of the world, and there is no division or contradiction; there is just the beautiful paradox of nondual awareness. A whole new dimension of spiritual maturity opens up to us at this level of awareness. Here, nothing is excluded, as everything, both dark and light, both form and formless, both mundane and transcendent, is seen to be an expression of oneness, and so nothing is avoided, denied, or feared. Even suffering itself is deeply embraced.

When full maturity has blossomed, the flower that bursts forth and opens into the light has to return to the darkness of the earth, thus fulfilling its divine destiny. You too are destined to return to the shady world of form after awakening to your inner light. It's the way of reality … and your denial or avoidance of it does not make it any less real.

COMPASSION: THE HEART OF REALITY

The return of awakeness from the lofty heights of the absolute perspective to the nitty gritty of the earthly experience sows the seeds of compassion. If you are fully awake and fully human, you will inevitably see that suffering is integral to the movement of life. Life includes the inevitability of birth and death. Whatever is born into a structure is unavoidably subject to the dissolution of that very structure, and this fact in itself is the cause of great terror. The fear of loss is at the root of Buddha's declaration that "life is suffering." Compassion cannot reveal itself without an unconditional understanding and acceptance of this truth.

Very often, there is confusion around the idea that "life is suffering." However, there's a big difference between a *story* of suffering and nakedly meeting what is there. Naked suffering is an unadulterated meeting with the raw reality of life: there is no sense of self in this, just an honest and wholehearted present-moment experience. The *story* of suffering is the manipulation of reality to conform with a preconceived idea of who you think you are. There is an egoic investment in the suffering, as in "poor me, this shouldn't have happened," or "bad things always happen to me, I'm unlucky." The identification with a victim-story cushions you from naked pain, building a fortress around the heart of being. You cannot be authentically free as long as you are defending yourself from the totality of life.

Perhaps you have come to a place of deep acceptance of the fact that suffering is part of the earthly experience. But, even in this acceptance, there can be confusion about the nature of compassion. Maybe you see that the constant movement of life, rising and falling, appearing and disappearing, has been a fact since the big bang gave birth to the universe.

Or that suffering has been going on and on from the beginning of time until the present moment. And maybe a profound question arises: "If suffering is endless, what is the point of compassion?" You may think that one little action toward change is like a drop in the ocean, so is it really worth it? Will it make any difference at all? The wisdom of empty mind says there is no point to taking action; life is *as it is*. But the wisdom of a full heart says that you have no choice but to respond if the impulse to respond is true in you. Compassion isn't about "doing good things." It's got nothing to do with charity or pity. It's got everything to do with something so much more radical and far-reaching than this: *it's the recognition of compassion as the heart of reality.*

True compassion means that the self is not invested in an outcome. In awakeness, "you" are not doing anything at all; the awakeness in you is simply being itself. Awakeness naturally moves toward the awakeness inherent in unawakeness, like a magnet that attracts its likeness. The light in you moves toward the darkness because herein lies the seed of light, where the unborn bud is poised to burst through. And although the bud of awakening is wonderfully transcendent, the flower of awakening is uncompromisingly immanent.

The unavoidable choice to face everything that is not yet awake, both within *you* and in the world, is the movement of awakeness. Along the way, you may meet a huge amount of suffering or you may meet very little; it doesn't matter either way. What matters is your unwavering willingness to meet this suffering all the way. This is not feeding the suffering but, instead, allowing consciousness to move through you according to divine will. It's what the Indian mystic and poet Rabindranath Tagore meant when he said, "To find God, you must welcome everything." In this willingness to unconditionally welcome every single thing in the field of your experience, you become a bodhisattva, dedicated to the illumination of all beings, one drop at a time. It's a choiceless choice.

THE POWER OF FORGIVENESS

The choice to meet suffering consciously, and then to open wider than this suffering, is the act of forgiveness. Very often there's an idea that forgiveness is something you *do*, perhaps a kind gesture, the writing of a "letter of forgiveness" to everyone who's ever hurt you, or a turning of the other cheek. But the action is really an inner one. It's the choice to open wider than you want to, wider than you can even imagine.

Sometimes, you can really believe that you're choosing to meet suffering consciously and yet somehow you're still a victim of this suffering. For example, when you're in the grip of a dark emotion and you feel it intensely, you think you're meeting it completely, yet it doesn't dissolve. The pain is like a rock; it just stays there. In this case, there's still a subtle refusal to let go of the victim story. To open wider than the suffering is to be willing for the victim to die. As much as you say you no longer want to be a victim, the death of this victim is synonymous with the death of self, because victim-identity is a primary part of the ego's scaffolding. The question to be faced here is this: "Who would you be without the victim?" This isn't to be replaced with another idea of self, not even a positive self! The question is one that functions to take you deeper into the core of being where there is no self, but only if you are willing for the structures that uphold your sense of self to come tumbling down.

Of course, when trauma runs deep, if you've been physically or emotionally abused by someone in your family, a stranger, or by a collective force (such as the Holocaust or political exile), it's difficult to forgive. After all, the abuse did take place and you were indeed a victim of someone else's violence, hatred, or insanity. Letting go of the victim story is certainly not about condoning injustice or cruelty; it's not about making a wrong right. It's really not about the "other," but about you. Holding on to "it shouldn't have happened" perpetuates a grievance. This creates an energetic contraction that freezes your life force, locks it into the past, and prevents full engagement with life now. One of the primary handicaps of trauma is the inability to "cope" with situations that invoke strong emotions. There's often a withdrawal from the deeper current of life, a closing down of the feeling-nature that shows up as an inability to be intimate (either emotionally or sexually), and a very high sensitivity to the stress of new situations, unexpected events, and loss. But even though this self-protective pattern continues way past the original event, it is possible for the energetic knot of trauma to be released.

Through having the courage to face what deeply hurts and "sitting inside it" without judgment, there is a dissolution of the grievance. It's precisely this "sitting inside the experience" that was not possible when the traumatic event originally happened. The resistance to the horror and pain of the original event created a kind of splitting off of consciousness as a form of protection, and then the overlay of a story that says, "This shouldn't be happening."

Forgiveness is, first and foremost, an inner journey. It's about *you*. Are you willing to put an end to your inner conflict? Are you willing to meet the violence, hatred, cruelty, injustice, unkindness, greed, and ignorance in you? Are you willing to see that each of us is capable of dark feelings? These feelings may or may not be acted on, but the point is that we are each capable of experiencing these feelings. Forgiveness is the natural outcome of letting go of inner conflict. It begins with taking responsibility for your inner experience rather than continuing to avoid the pain by throwing it outward through blame and retaliation.

The power of forgiveness is poignantly encapsulated in *The Railway Man*, the autobiographical story of Eric Lomax, a prisoner of war in World War II who suffered brutal torture at the hands of the Japanese.[3] This experience left deeply buried emotional scars in his psyche that created havoc in his personal life. Many years later, after uncovering in himself a desire for revenge, he set out to kill his former tormentor. But in meeting him and pouring out his story of pain and hatred, he saw at the same time the humanity within his tormentor and the inhumanity within himself. As his heart opened, his inner reality was transformed and a tender friendship developed between the two men that lasted until they both passed away in old age.

At the core of every human being is a desire for love and wholeness: all acts of terror and horror are misguided attempts to find this. When you are the one who has been hurt by these terrorizing and horrifying acts, it may seem like it's impossible to believe this. Each one of us is called to dig much deeper into our inner knowing, to see that when the desire for love and wholeness moves through a form that has also suffered and been damaged, it comes out in distorted ways. At the root of this distortion is an ignorance of true nature and a consequent acting from a belief in separation. From this belief, all fear, hatred, violence in the name of justice, and other endless harmful acts are inevitable. Seeing that ignorance is the root cause of all suffering opens our hearts. We see but do not judge; we see without a story. This is the essence of compassion, redemption, and resurrection. As Jesus said as he was dying on the cross: "Forgive them Father for they know not what they do."[4]

An open heart allows the forgiveness of others, the world, life, God, and of the self. In choosing to open to the mystery of this moment with all its horror, you, as a separate self, die in this moment as it is, and what is revealed is the unending glory of an inner power. Forgiveness has the power to heal, for your sake and for the sake of the world. It's a power that defies all opposition. And it's more potent than any action.

LOVE IN ACTION

Whether we call it the power of forgiveness, the power of wholeness, or the power of God, what we're really talking about here is the power of real love. We often think of love as something nice, kind, or pleasurable. But there is nothing fluffy about real love, and it certainly doesn't conform to any of our ideas of how love should feel or behave.

Real love is radical. It is gentle yet fierce, tenacious yet selfless, unconditional yet uncompromising. Just like a mother, love gets the job done even when it's unpleasant. And just like a mother, she will do anything to protect her children; she'll even sacrifice herself. When things get tough, love is unafraid of getting her hands dirty in the cesspool of earthly life. Love has the fortitude to go into the dirty places—business, banking, politics, the food and pharmaceutical industries, the medical establishment, and even religion.

There is no experience on the earthly dimension that this love does not embrace. This love loves everything. This love loves this moment exactly as it is. This love loves the human experience. It loves the multitextured tapestry of life. It loves every wave of phenomenal appearance, even the pain, limitation, resistance, and the stuckness—all of it! It loves the experience of growth and transformation, when a physical, emotional, or mental stuckness moves to *un*stuckness, when an energetic contraction is released, and when life shifts from limitation to liberation. We expect awakening to be a state in which there is no movement, no growth, no transformation; a place of unchanging stillness in which nothing happens. But awakening allows all of it, both the untouchable stillness at the core of being and the unpredictable movement of life's energies, because it is all an experience of the one beingness that is at the core of everything. Love rejoices in the both the beauty and the horror of it all!

What is different about awakened consciousness is the very real sense that it is not *you* who is making the movement happen. The sense of ownership of the movement of life is simply no longer there. Instead, there is a *willingness* for movement to happen, an innocent inquiry or curiosity into what is here in this present-moment experience without trying to fix or change this moment. It's a kind of "effortless effort," a collaboration between awareness and life that simply and divinely allows movement to happen. This effortless movement is love in action.

Love in action has no vestige of self-investment in it. Rather, it's an action that serves the wholeness of life. The dynamic power of this love is transformative. In the willingness to enter the heart of darkness, that place where personal fear, horror, terror, and pain are the greatest, there is the potential for rebirth into the universal heart, the place where everything, both dark and light, is seen to be an expression of oneness. Love in action is an outpouring of the wisdom of emptiness. Rooted in the unbounded nature of things, yet refusing to be lopsidedly identified with the unmovable ground of being as another spiritual concept, love allows the river of compassion to pour into those places starved of light. The beggar, the thief, the murderer, the terrorist, the deformed, and the sick are all worthy receptacles of love's fulfillment.

Sometimes the action that is required is an *inner* action, the conscious choice to turn attention inward to the source of everything as stillness. And sometimes what is required is an *outer* action that has an impact on the phenomenal world: a word spoken or letter written, a touch or some other material comfort given, a tree planted, or a shelter built. What's important here is that this action is not a reaction of the seeking mind and its incessantly horizontal movement. Love in action is a movement that rises up out of the stillness of being. It has no agenda of pleasure or comfort-seeking, nor of pain aversion. Neither does it have an agenda of what the outcome of this movement should look like. Love simply moves, because movement is its nature. Love is the movement of innate intelligence through our earthly lives. It's love that calls you to awaken, that sparks the fire of truth and provides the momentum for you to face the abyss of being, even though fear rears its head in all directions. And it's also love that informs you to take care of the physical vehicle you inhabit while here on earth, that moves you to care for the body of the planet and all her living inhabitants as if they were your own children. Real love allows you to recognize that all life is connected and that there is no separation between inner and outer worlds. Without this love, all worlds become dry and lifeless.

This kind of love is illogical to the egoic mind that likes to package love as a commodity. Ego cannot conceive of real love because love is unknowable by the mind. It's even unknowable by the heart, because most often when we speak of the heart, we're referring to the *emotional* heart. Both mind and heart are tainted by our conditioned responses to life and so neither can see clearly. Only when the mind and heart have dissolved into the emptiness of being can real love be fully recognized and expressed. Real love is not blind. Real love can see right into the heart of reality, because love *is* the heart of reality. And this love is inseparable from the awakeness inherent in all living things.

While the density of certain structures, both physical and psychological, may seem insurmountable, disintegration of these structures is inevitable when the seeds of awakened consciousness take root, one person at a time. Of course, we cannot possibly know the outcome; perhaps a collapse into total Armageddon or even oblivion is inevitable. But the point is that love is unafraid to go there. Love does not see money as evil, only how it is used. Love does not see business as evil, only the way it operates. Love sees that it is the ignorance of our true nature as wholeness that causes all earthly devastation. When you, too, have polished the lens of your heart and your mind, you will see clearly. And you will see that the love in you is inseparable from the awakeness in all things. The vision to penetrate into the heart of reality means there is an inevitable taking care of what needs to be taken care of, and this includes your body and the body of the planet, even though both of these will eventually die. This is right action.

It's time for an intelligent dialogue that includes worldly actions in awakened perception. It starts with you. And as long as you're alive, it never ends. Because you, in the very aliveness of *this* moment, are the vehicle through which love can recognize itself and give birth to the light of conscious awareness.

CHAPTER 6

Your Role In the Birth of a New Humanity

HEAVEN ON EARTH

Perhaps you can now recognize how important *you* are to the evolution of consciousness. Without you, the world would not exist, because there would be no mechanism of conscious awareness through which to perceive it. As long as you're alive in physical form, you and the world are inseparable. When asked by his disciples when the Kingdom of Heaven would arrive, Jesus replied: "The Kingdom of Heaven is spread upon the Earth, but men do not see it."[5] The intention of this statement was to unveil that heaven and earth are not separate, although they appear to be so to the unenlightened mind.

Heaven is an inner dimension of consciousness: the pure light of spirit. Enlightenment is the discovery of this invisible sanctuary as the core of who you are and the core of everything. It's the discovery of the eternal presence that existed prior to the birth of the universe and continues to exist in this moment. It's also what is here before thinking arises in you.

This dimension of absolute reality is deathless, it has no beginning and no ending. It is the wide-open space of emptiness. Yet it is fully awake.

Everything that exists is born from and dies into this emptiness. Each physical and each psychological form—every star, grain of sand, cell, atom, beggar, king, thought, and feeling—arises out of this eternal ground of being. Ever since the big bang, something continues to emerge out of nothing. Manifest reality, the outer visible world, is a never-ending expression of consciousness. Another way of saying it is: earth is a reflection of heaven. When we contemplate natural forms, especially those that have a quality of lightness or spaciousness, such as a flower, a crystal, a raindrop, the ocean, the sky, or the cosmos, we come closest to a clear reflection of the radiance of heaven. These life-forms emanate and inspire in us the qualities of beauty, grace, freedom, and stillness. In all these manifestations, there is an innocence and purity that transcends thinking.

With the birth of humanity came the capacity to create new forms that serve a practical purpose, such as tools for hunting, clothes for warmth, and structures for shelter, as well as forms that serve to uplift the soul, such as art and sacred objects. At the same time came the birth of a new psychological form: the sense of self or ego. As our minds developed in complexity, so did our capacity to create ever more wondrous and ever more horrendous forms: vehicles to transport us from A to B, rockets that fly to outer space, microscopes that reveal the mysteries of atomic space, phones and computers that connect us in the blink of an eye, and sophisticated weapons of unimaginable atrocity. As the ego's self-protection mechanism has become more entrenched over time, we have also become increasingly distanced from the original sanctity of our radiant core. Today, our earth has, for the most part, become a reflection of the hell of our own unawakened minds.

With the very real possibility of total planetary annihilation, many more people are wondering how we can save the world from this hell. It's tempting to want to *do* something to stop those whom we believe are responsible for the dramatic disturbances to the economic, political, social, and climactic status quo. And it's natural to respond with kindness, care, and generosity to those who are suffering as a result of these upheavals. While we may be able to sometimes help ease the pain of sentient beings with attention and money, or initiate humanitarian change through campaigning, we can't save the world by hating those who do harm or by fighting for what we want. It is only love that can erase the hate, and only peace that can stop the war. Neither love nor peace are commodities to be found in the visible world.

Salvation comes when you see the love and the peace that are already here beyond and beneath form. It's not a denial of the relative reality of form, but rather it is a deeper seeing. As soon as form is born, whether it be physical or psychological, there is separation. It cannot be any other way. This is the nature of things, but you have a choice. You can choose to focus your attention on the surface and conclude that separation is the only reality, or you can choose to penetrate the surface reality through to the deeper dimension within, where all form appears and disappears.

Salvation is seeing the light that is available to you when you rest, right *here*, in the timeless, formless ground of being. You *see* the light because you *are* the light: this is oneness. There is so much more power in this than in separation. Only the oneness in you can see the oneness at the radiant core of existence. Only the love in you can see the love within your enemy. Only the peace in you can see the peace within the storm. Only the God in you can see God in everything.

Whatever you do or don't do, you're constantly transmitting like a beacon. You're either transmitting oneness or separation. You can't help it; your state of consciousness sends out a signal whether or not you are aware of it. You can be doing good things but transmitting conflict because you have not recognized your true nature as peace. The world has many well-intentioned people like this, but there is no real long-range effectiveness in their actions. Only when the light in you sees the light of awakeness in everyone and everything can there be real change.

When Mother Teresa was asked how she could continue feeding, touching, and giving comfort to the diseased, crippled, mentally ill, and abandoned as they lay dying in wretched conditions, she replied: "It's not hard, because in each one of them I see Jesus in one of his more distressing disguises." Mother Teresa worked tirelessly to relieve the suffering of those in desperate circumstances. The massive impact of her mission on the psyche of religious and secular society is testament to the power of the Christ-light that had awakened within her heart. In awakening, you can be still and do nothing, or you can move and take action; either way, you are a beacon of light unto yourself and unto the world.

It has been predicted that Christ will return to earth to usher in a new era of peace and love. The return of Christ is not the appearance of one person who will save us from our troubles, but the birth of light that is happening within each of us as we awaken out of the dream of separation. It is this light that is now birthing a new humanity through you.

AN UNCONDITIONAL RELATIONSHIP TO LIFE

When the light of awakeness has been turned on in your heart and mind all the way, not just as a state that comes and goes, you cannot fail to recognize yourself *as* love and you recognize that love is all there is. Everything that exists is love—not as a story in your mind, a memory, dream, or fantasy, but as the fullness of your direct experience of this present moment. The beautiful paradox is that the emptiness of consciousness within, which is where this love is experienced, is also love. The capacity to embrace this paradox takes you to a radical acceptance of *what is*, a wide-open space within where all division between inner and outer, light and dark, spirit and matter dissolves. This is the reality of oneness.

The idea of oneness is extremely attractive. It stretches out its hand and offers the salve of heart connection, like-mindedness, community, and peace. It conjures up the dream of a paradisiacal world in which all differences, disagreements, and darkness have been eradicated. For many people, it paints a picture of a world in which we are free to enjoy the Garden of Eden, joining hands, gazing into one another's eyes, and telling one another "I love you."

We can create all kinds of stories in our minds about what oneness looks like, but as long as each of these stories remains unquestioned, the truth of oneness cannot reveal itself. So many people who believe in oneness, although sincere in their belief, lack the true power to contribute to a new world because they fail to investigate their own unilluminated thinking.

As long as you deny any movement of energy within yourself that you deem wrong, bad, or unacceptable, such as rage, despair, or lust, you deny the movement of life: this is not oneness. Perhaps you hold a perspective in which all politicians, corporations, religions, atheists, and rich people are evil, but as long as you reject a proportion of the world's population for being wrong, bad, or unacceptable, you reject the full expression of life, and this is not oneness. You may be morally, politically, or spiritually correct, but wearing the badge of "oneness" without an open-ended inquiry into what is true easily becomes another calcified belief that prolongs the war between us and them. I'm not talking here about acting out on your rage, despair, or lust, or condoning harmful actions taken by those whose agenda is not aligned to humanity's upliftment. I'm referring to an awakened relationship to life that brings an end to separation.

Every part of you that separates itself from the totality of life gets projected onto someone or something. Since nothing can be excluded from the *totality* of life, meaning that everything is included, it has to express itself somehow and somewhere. The first law of thermodynamics (the science of how energy is exchanged) states that nothing can be created or destroyed. If it can't exist in you because you deny or reject it, then it has to exist in someone or something else. This is good news for the ego—as long as this wrongness/darkness is "out there," then the separate sense of "me" can continue to survive. But this is bad news for the world, because the world cannot right itself unless *you* right yourself. This is why *you* are so important: not you as the separate self, but you as the awakened consciousness that dissolves all separation.

Your willingness to examine, with excruciating honesty, what is assumed to be separate from the totality of life crucifies all that is false in you. Every notion of self that prevents you from knowing the wholeness of your being will come tumbling down. Every concept of oneness that prevents you from seeing that darkness and light are inseparable will fall apart. Every idea and imagination that does not recognize the source of everything that exists in your present-moment experience will be brought to the fire of truth to be illuminated. This includes every thought, feeling, and emotion that you have ever pushed away. Anything you have banished into the shadows will come running toward you to be fully met within the light of awakened awareness and welcomed into the radiant openness of your true nature.

If you're sincere in your desire for freedom, you will not turn away from that which scares you, repulses you, or threatens to crush you. You've done this a million times before. Perhaps this time you will choose an inconceivable yes to the waves of phenomenal existence—whether they appear as terror, anguish, or inexplicable bliss—without drowning in them or losing yourself in the story told by the ever-changing tides of life. Perhaps this time you will be vigilant enough to see what really dies and what remains when it is invited into the luminosity of awareness.

The exciting possibility here is the end of all stories of victimhood. This ending results in an unconditional relationship to life in which you choose to meet suffering consciously, and then choose to open wider than this suffering. This is the resurrection: a falling into the unboundedness of love that recognizes itself in everything. As the Indian saint Neem Karoli Baba said: "I love suffering, it brings me closer to God."[6]

Conscious suffering is the decision to walk with resolute presence and unadulterated openness through every inner and outer landscape and to recognize that which is true beneath and beyond all appearances. In conscious suffering, every step is a crucifixion and a resurrection. This is the razor's edge of true awakening in which the archaic mechanism of ego is given up in service to that which is real and you are reborn as that which you truly are.

When everything false in you dies, what remains is the truth of love. Not a kind love or a polite love. Not a love tied up in a pink bow or in red frilly knickers. But a love that is uncompromising in its inclusion of the totality of life. This love cannot be packaged, it cannot be bought or sold or negotiated with. It is limitless, unconditional, wild, and absolutely free. This love is in the heart of you, every saint and sinner, and in every speck of gold dust and piece of dirt.

When this love is seen *as* the heart of *everything,* an inexplicable recognition of nonduality within duality arises. This is the ultimate cosmic joke that resounds across the universe as the "peace that passeth all understanding." When that unconditional laugh lands in your belly, the ripples of transformation in your life have begun.

THE EMBODIMENT OF AWAKENING

Perhaps, having absorbed the words thus far, you can now fully recognize that awakening is just the beginning and that the embodiment of this awakening is the real journey. Awakening itself is simple. Of course, from the point of view of the ego it's not so simple, because the ego, being time-oriented, has an investment in enlightenment as a future goal. But once the mind recognizes itself as radiant emptiness, then awakening is absolutely natural and effortless. It's as inevitable as a flower blooming from a bud. And yet, while the realization of the absolute truth of emptiness in which a separate "me" does not exist is undoubtedly a profoundly transformative experience, living this truth is frequently more of a challenge.

The adventure begins not in the rarified atmosphere of transcendence, but in the midst of the chaos of life. Living the truth of awakening has never been more of an imperative than in today's rapidly changing world. Many of us live complex, multifaceted lives with jobs, careers, financial responsibilities, relationships, and families. Some of us are also attempting to pursue our dreams or live our highest potential, and make a contribution (however small or large) to the world. At the same time, we're increasingly aware that over half the planet's population lives in abject poverty and horrifying circumstances. Somehow, all of this needs to be included in our awakening.

If awakening is to be complete in you, if it's to be a *radical* awakening, it must become alive in every cell of your being. Your beingness must sing and dance with the discovery of its light-essence. As this light filters out from the mind into the heart and further into the density of physical form, there's a purification of all that is not yet living the truth of this awakeness. This is where it gets tricky. This is where the ancient movement of ego wants to claim ownership of the light, where it wants to hold on to an image of awakening as a transcendent, positive, blissful, or never-ending experience. Purification means that everything that is unconscious in you will be brought to the fire of awakeness to be transformed. This is where confusion, doubt, and fear come in. You may think "surely if I'm enlightened, I shouldn't be having these unenlightened thoughts or these painful feelings." It's at this point that there is a danger of reidentification with the story of your life. But it's exactly at this point that the invitation to the greatest adventure holds out its hand to you. Right here in *this* moment, and in each moment as it unfolds (whether it is an enlightened or an unenlightened moment), you are invited to rest more deeply within and to willingly open to the divine mystery and mess of that which we call the human experience.

If you choose to be unequivocal in taking up this invitation (remember there is no halfway), your life will no longer be your own but will be given in service to this invitation. If you are radically sincere in your surrender to awakeness, the light of your innermost being will come rushing to meet your outermost expression, and everything that stands in the way of this truth will be dismantled. In some people, this happens like a meandering river that gently but persistently reaches its destination. In others, this happens like a tidal wave that obliterates anything fragile or weak in its path. Either way, if the demolition job is thorough, an incredible silence will emanate from your core and reverberate through your environment, community, culture, and world. This silence is your true power, because it is inseparable from the silent core of creation. It is the same as the light of God. The embodiment of this light is the start of authentic living and it has the power to give birth to a new world.

This new world starts in your mind as the discovery of that which is awake in you. This is the foundation and nothing radically new can be created without this. It's a fundamental shift in perception. Before the discovery, you see through the myopic eyes of the ego-mind (100 percent me-centered), and after the discovery, your vision is unclouded like a clear sky, without a center. The former is a prison; the latter is a sanctuary of light without boundaries.

This awakening out of the illusion of a separate self is often recognized in the midst of intense suffering. It's as if the self-referencing mind has no escape route and collapses in on itself. Most often, this is experienced as a glimpse of a transcendent reality in which there is no suffering. It's the realization of emptiness as the ground of reality—what we may call a nondual awareness.

As you inevitably move out of the sanctuary of the enlightened mind to navigate the hustle and bustle of everyday life, this nondual awareness is given the opportunity to descend into the fullness of the heart. A deeper surrender is called for here. This is where awakening stops being a mental realization and starts being a living expression. In the crucible of the heart, love demands everything. This love will overturn every stone to reveal that which is still hiding in the shadows of self-defense. It will dig out everything that remains unloved in you and reflect this back to you through the mirror of relationship. It will push your buttons to test that which is still unconscious in you. Every whisper of previously unmet emotion will be dragged to the surface to be purged in the uncompromising glare of love's eyes. It's an unrelenting spiritual catharsis that demands a deeper opening and willingness to be vulnerable. Radical awakening sows the seeds of transparent communication, genuine communion, and co-creative growth; in other words, authentic relating. This is the basis of true community, of *sangha*, not of like-mindedness but of open-heartedness. This community includes not only our human brothers and sisters but also every living entity, from the tiniest microbe to the vastness of planet Earth.

Most often we overlook that our bodies are also a part of this community. In fact, the body is not really a single entity but a community of cells. Each cell in the body is a world unto itself and is subject to the same mechanisms that govern all living systems. Consider that a cell can be either enlightened or "endarkened." Also consider the possibility that an enlightened cell is one that functions at its highest potential to create optimum well-being (scientists have found that cells hold light in the form of biophotons). And, consider the possibility that an "endarkened" cell is one whose inherent light-filled nature is obscured by physical and emotional toxicity, which leads to stress and dis-ease. Almost all spiritual traditions, including modern-day teachings, avoid any real conversation about the relationship between the body and consciousness and instead emphasize total disidentification with physical form. But as we move into a new paradigm of oneness, the recognition of the body as a temple for consciousness can no longer be ignored. Radical awakening calls us to dissolve the boundary between matter and spirit and to embrace the possibility of cellular awakening as the cornerstone of conscious living. To do so is to embody the mystery of the divine within all manifestations.

When you embrace this mystery, the mystery starts to move through you. Your life is no longer your own but is given in service to the light. This isn't just a nice spiritual idea but a very tangible and powerful new way of living. When awakening is fully embodied, you simply can't help it; service becomes the overriding motivation for being alive. It's not about "being good" but about "being God." It's your true nature to operate as divinity; and the conscious recognition of this is the fulfillment of your true life's purpose. This is when your inner destiny of awakening to the truth of who you are aligns with your outer destiny of expressing this awakeness through your actions. Your doing is no longer a byproduct of the ego's survival mechanism; rather, it is an outpouring of the brilliance at your radiant core. Essentially, you become the eyes, ears, hands, feet, heart, and voice of God. You live your greatness through the work you do, whether this work is sweeping the floor, building a house, writing a book, managing a multi-million-dollar company, or bringing up a child. It's not *what* you do but *how* you do it that makes all the difference.

If awakening is to serve a real purpose in our lives, it needs to find new forms of expression through our everyday interactions. And if this awakening is to serve a purpose in the bigger picture of birthing a new humanity, it needs to engage us fully with the evolutionary impulse of existence. Enlightenment is no longer a secret reserved for mystics, nor a luxury indulged in by privileged westerners seeking to become "more spiritual." Awakening is a necessity if we are to survive and thrive. If enlightenment is to be of any use, it needs to come down from the mountaintop and get its hands dirty in the marketplace of human affairs. It's an uncompromising embracing of both the waves of phenomenal expression and the ocean of inner stillness that brings us into deep intimacy with the creative force of life. This deep intimacy doesn't mean you get lost in the story of the world, but it *does* mean you're willing to wholeheartedly meet the world without a story.

The mystic and spiritual teacher Osho often talked about this embodied awakeness as the process of becoming "Zorba the Buddha." In other words, the new evolutionary human being is someone who is utterly anchored within the light of awakened nature, yet passionately committed to the bittersweet juiciness of earthly existence. The absolute truth is "you are not your body," but your direct experience will show that your body is here moving through consciousness every time you walk or run or jump. The truth is "there is no self," but you answer when your name is called. Yes, the truth is "you do not exist and neither do I," but it makes a difference in your quality of life whether you see and hear with openheartedness rather than with judgment.

Authentic awakening is not static; it's a fresh moment-to-moment awareness of that which is unfolding within our direct experience. And what's unfolding for so many of us within contemporary culture is an increasing complexity, interconnectivity, and creativity at an exponential rate. Today, we have the opportunity to become so much more than previous generations had ever dreamt of. For most of us, there are more resources, technologies, information, and wisdom available to us than ever before.

An enlightened world can only become a reality if collective consciousness radically transforms. Waiting for salvation from some external power (whether this be a political or spiritual or cosmic or even divine power) is a fantasy that postpones the very transformation we seek. The responsibility for change lies with each of us. It's about each one of us absolutely living the truth of awakening in our everyday lives ... here and now.

PART THREE

LIVING THE TRUTH

OF AWAKENING IN

EVERYDAY LIFE

CHAPTER 7

Looking For Wholeness Through Another

THE WILLINGNESS TO EXPOSE THE TRUTH OF RELATIONSHIP

Living the truth of awakening in the midst of everyday relationships is where the rubber really hits the road. Despite already recognizing the separate "me" as an illusory construct, you still drown in the waves of intense emotion when your buttons are pushed. Buttons usually get pushed when you are in close emotional or physical proximity to someone, whether it be a spouse, family member, friend, coworker, neighbor, or spiritual teacher.

I have met many longtime spiritual seekers who have glimpsed the clarity of nondual awareness, as well as those who are newer to the path of self-inquiry, and the same questions are asked over and over again. Questions such as, "I've realized the absolute truth of oneness, so why do I still feel so alone and disconnected from my husband/my wife/my friends/my family?" or "I know I am no-body and no-thing, so why do I still feel rejected/unloved/hurt when my mother/my father/my sister/my brother/my boss doesn't recognize who I really am?" Other common questions are: "If I awaken, will the pain and conflict in my relationship go away?" or "If I awaken, will I find the perfect relationship/my soul mate/the one for me?" and "If I awaken, does that mean my relationship will come to an end and I'll be all alone again?"

Living the truth of awakening in the midst of everyday relationships is often very challenging and confusing for spiritual seekers. But it's also where there is the greatest potential for a deepening of spiritual maturity and embodiment. It's in the messy marketplace of human interactions that the clear light of awakened consciousness is given the opportunity to filter down into the shadowy recesses of the heart, where it can encounter and dissolve any energetic contractions that limit the fullness of love.

How and why awakening transforms intimate relationship is the raw edge of spiritual inquiry, because it's where most traditional spiritual teachings refuse to go and it demands a radical self-exposure. This self-exposure is the willingness to uncover all mental and emotional acrobatics that are a distraction from seeing yourself as you really are in the mirror of relationship. It's also the willingness to leave no stone unturned in uprooting the core belief in separation that drives all seeking, including the seeking of wholeness through relationship.

If this willingness to expose all hiding places, safety precautions, and cozy concepts is truly alive in you, even if it means the end of your dream of fulfillment through relationship, then you are invited to stand at the raw edge of awakening and be a pioneer of a new conversation in spirituality. It's a radically honest dialogue in which you both *tell* the truth and *listen* to the truth. This truth is not necessarily the ultimate truth, the absolute truth, or any other kind of spiritually correct truth. The radical dialogue offered here is a much vaster vista than any of this. While pointing unwaveringly to the luminous truth of untarnished awakeness, this dialogue includes every twist and turn of personal truth, every buried feeling of rejection, doubt, frustration, and sadness, every unexpressed longing for intimacy and fulfillment, and every previously unexamined belief that attempts to cover up the black hole of aloneness.

Are you ready to discover what is more real than any of your cherished ideas about love and relationship? Are you willing to stop looking for wholeness through another and instead discover what is already whole, here and now? Perhaps the invitation to discover what is already whole is familiar to you—it is often spoken about in spiritual circles. And maybe it sounds obvious to stop looking outside yourself for something that you already are. But, as your experience probably indicates, it's often much more difficult to embody this truth than you imagine, especially when it comes to the raw reality of everyday relationships.

Despite the twists and turns involved in uncovering the truth of relationship, the layers of protection wrapped around the tenderness of your heart, and any resistance in letting go of your cherished dreams, are you truly willing to start this conversation? If your answer is a resounding yes, then let's dive in with an honest investigation into the central myth of relationship.

THE MYTH OF THE SPECIAL RELATIONSHIP

The idea of a special relationship that will complete us is a universal one. Almost every single person alive today—whether they are conscious of it or not—believes (or hopes) that there's a perfect partner, a soul mate, or "the one" they can share their life with. Although it's often silenced by layers of social, cultural, and religious conditioning, this belief exists even in cultures where arranged marriages are the norm. It also exists in those who are "happily single" and are either actively or passively avoiding relationship. This avoidance is rarely a conscious choice; rather, it's likely to be driven by the fear of disappointment or hurt when it all goes wrong. The idea of a special relationship is also very commonly projected onto a spiritual teacher, as "the one" who will finally remove all obstacles and bestow enlightenment, and therefore provide the ultimate completeness.

Let's take a pause right here. I invite you to be still ... and in this stillness to find out if there's any movement in you either *toward* relationship (perhaps you experience this as a yearning in your heart or a feeling of emptiness in your belly or a tug toward someone real or imagined) or *away from* relationship (perhaps you experience this as a slight closure in your heart or a shield around your belly or a repulsion toward the idea of commitment or intimacy). If there is any movement at all, however faint or subtle, then the idea of a special relationship is functioning in you. There's really nothing wrong with this idea; after all, relationship is central to the human experience. But if this idea remains unexamined, the full depth of embodied awakeness will elude you. What actually needs to be examined here is not whether relationship itself has any validity in an awakened life—although this *is* a vital part of the inquiry—but that the search for fulfillment through relationship is an utter misdirection of attention if true fulfillment is to be found.

I invite you now to take another pause ... and to consider that the search for the perfect partner, soul mate, or "the one" is exactly the same as the search for enlightenment. Consider that both the search for the special relationship *and* the search for enlightenment carry the same hope (that there's no more painful or difficult feelings to disturb your happiness) and the same dream (that you will become whole, complete, finally fulfilled). Also consider that they both contain the same delusions (that you will rise above the messiness of the world and live a perfect life) and the same obstacles (the refusal to integrate shadow aspects of self and the subtle identification with a spiritual or "special" ego). Could it be that the enduring and alluring myth of special relationship, just like the myth of enlightenment, is precisely what stands in the way of true fulfillment?

If you've been on the path of spiritual inquiry for some time, it's very likely that you understand (at least in your mind) how the seeking mechanism itself perpetuates the spiritual search, so that awakening or enlightenment is always a future destination. This conversation has been alive in spiritual circles for many years. But when it comes to the search for fulfillment through relationship, this seeking mechanism is mostly overlooked or ignored. Somehow, it's just too painful to let go of the dream of finding the special relationship. And yet it's the same seeking mechanism that drives all seeking, whether it be the need to accumulate wealth, the insatiable hunger for power, the addiction to a substance-induced high, or the craving for sugary foods.

The seeking mechanism is a part of ego's primary and utterly natural function of ensuring the survival of the human species. In its rightful role as the driver for procreation, it expresses itself as sexual impulse. The horizontal movement—from perceived lack to perceived fulfillment and from disillusionment to the longing and search for fulfillment—is a perfect operating system when it comes to the fulfillment of the desire for sex. If we are to reproduce as earthly forms, the sexual act must be repeated, over and over again. In this case, it's not a one-time affair but a continual cycle of craving and satisfaction. Because the satisfaction is temporary, the cycle continues. Fueled by a flood of hormones, this seeking is an unconscious biological necessity. But when this cyclical system hijacks the deeper spiritual longing for the remembrance of wholeness, it fails.

The fallacy is that it sets up all sorts of mental and emotional projections onto reality, creating a fantasy that this longing can be satisfied by something in the external world of form. Mostly this takes the form of a prized possession (it could be as simple as a coveted pair of shoes or as sophisticated as winning the Nobel Peace Prize), a person to whom we are attracted (it could be the pop-star/actor we worship or the boy/girl next door), a drug (chemical or plant-based) that promises nirvana, or a vision of personal (or global) utopia. The object of desire then becomes something we must *have* at all cost, and so we become devoted to this chase, even if it takes a lifetime. But the seeking mechanism itself, whether it be the search for fulfillment through fame, fortune, chocolate, relationship, or enlightenment, is the very thing that unwittingly sabotages the fulfillment it seeks. If you investigate more closely, you'll see that the search for fulfillment is really a wild goose chase. It's a futile pursuit, because it's like chasing a phantom that cannot be possessed. This phantom is the dream of salvation, a perfect place (and time) where you are perfectly happy and nothing bad or painful happens. But this place does not exist, except in your imagination. And it's never the right time, because it's always in the future.

Even though the search for the special relationship seems so real and your whole life seems to depend on it, it actually takes you farther away from real completeness. If what you want is true fulfillment, and you can honestly say that you want this more than you want to hold onto your cherished idea of special relationship, then the incessant search for something outside yourself to give you what you think you want must come to a full stop. If what you really want is the end of suffering, your allegiance must be turned away from the horizontality of egoic satisfaction, once and for all.

True awakening invites you to devote yourself irrevocably, in every moment, to the discovery of wholeness in the vertical dimension of being. This does not necessarily mean that if you wish to awaken, you should turn away from relationship. On the contrary, it means that there is a deeper purpose to relationship. Awakening is not the end of relationship, but it *is* the end of the dream of relationship.

THE FALLACY OF SEEKING LOVE

If you've ever fallen in love, you'll remember how time seems to stand still, all your worries go away, and everything seems so alive. It feels like "coming home," because falling in love is a cessation of seeking. In finding the object of your dream, the search comes to a stop. In other words, the horizontal movement of egoic mind comes to a standstill and relaxes into the present moment. In this presence, you relax into the innate wholeness of being.

The hope and expectation is that this sense of wholeness will last forever, especially if you have found the perfect partner, your soul mate, or "the one." But this hope remains a dream if the seeking mechanism has not been fully exposed. Suffering is inevitable when the honeymoon period ends and the seeking starts again. For some, the bliss of wholeness lasts for several months, for others it is weeks, and for others it is just days. Now the dream becomes a drama. You either stay in the relationship, confused and hurt that there is conflict, and secretly (or overtly) try to change the other to fit the image of the perfect partner you fell in love with at the start of the relationship. Or you leave, believing you made a mistake and this wasn't the special relationship after all, and you put your efforts into looking for the "real" special relationship. This addiction to falling in love, without the honest inquiry into what drives this addictive movement, is why divorce and serial partnerships are so prevalent.

If what you really want is *real* love, not the dream (or the drama) of falling in love (and falling out of love), then not only does the fallacy of the seeking mechanism need to be exposed, but so does a more deeply rooted error: the belief that you exist as a separate entity. This belief is entrenched in the human psyche. It's the universal core wound of separation, as consciousness descends into form and forgets itself. Perhaps because it is such an ancient imprint, it has far-reaching repercussions on our daily interactions, whether it be with someone close to us, someone we have occasional contact with, a stranger on the other side of the world, or a spiritual teacher.

The core belief that you exist as a separate entity kick-starts a whole cascade of erroneous perceptions that filter into our collective language and behavior. When we say, "I love you," "I love chocolate," or "I love art," or even "I love truth," we have already divided existence into subject and object. Of course, this is an acceptable and convenient way to express ourselves in the relative reality of everyday life. But the way we communicate, if unexamined, remains a mass hypnosis that keeps us imprisoned in the dream of separation. The suffering comes because the radiant wholeness of your true nature (and everyone else's nature) cannot be unveiled within this dream, and the fullness of real love cannot then permeate your experience.

From the perspective of a separate self, that which is outside you (the object) is seen to be the cause of love and wholeness in you (the subject). As long as that something outside you—whether that something is a person, commodity, foodstuff, an artwork, or even a spiritual belief—gives you the version of love that matches your image of love, you feel content, fulfilled, and complete. In other words, you feel loved and you feel loving, and so you act in a friendly, kind, forgiving, and generous way toward the other. But as soon as that something stops giving you what you want, or it is taken away from you, you feel rejected, abandoned, deprived, punished, empty, alone, unfulfilled, and incomplete. You feel unloved and you stop being loving ... and so you automatically act in an unfriendly, unforgiving, unkind, and ungenerous way toward the other.

The *you* that you *think* you are, the conglomerate of conditioned mental and emotional responses we call the ego, has an army of strategies to deal with the perceived withdrawal of love. The ego will bully, blame, beg, barter, seduce, and pretend in order to get what it wants. Some of these strategies are overt, such as the power games ("I'm right, you're wrong") that result in arguments, tantrums, emotional violence, and, when taken to the extreme, physical violence. Other strategies are more covert, such as an almost imperceptible but constant nagging, an emotional frostiness, or playing the pleaser. Sometimes the strategy is even more concealed, such as when the importance of external appearances (physical beauty, strength/prowess, expensive clothing, worldly success/status, and so on) is amplified and used as a kind of bait for love.

Whatever strategy is employed, it's an attempt to control the uncontrollable. It's a demand on life to give you what you want. What most people want, whether they are conscious of it or not, is to feel loved, because feeling loved is the primordial memory of connectedness, belonging, and of being held in our mother's womb. It makes us feel safe and wanted. There's really nothing wrong with this, except that, if the deeper abyss of aloneness remains covered up by layers of strategy aimed at getting a sense of wholeness from outside of ourselves, there can only be a facsimile of love's true fulfillment. What most people call "love" is a fleeting experience that is a pale imitation of the enduring nature of real love.

BEYOND LOVE AND HATE

Real love, not the mind-created image of love, is not conditional on your emotional demands, your wishful thinking, nor on the contortions of your behavior. Real love is uncontrollable and is free of all conditions. This untamable love is what you glimpse when you fall in love. Only when the self-created fantasy of love temporarily disappears can a true love without limits reveal itself. It's a love without content—without subject or object—that allows an alive intimacy, or what we may call the experience of oneness.

This open space without content—without a "me" or a "you"—is incredibly scary to the egoic mind, whose function it is to categorize, compare, differentiate, and label. As the ego scrambles to make sense of the uncontainable mystery of love, it fabricates a story of what love is. The specifics of this story are based on personal, social, cultural, and karmic conditioning, and it revolves around what makes "you" feel good, safe, or special. The story may go as follows: *When you give me love, I feel good, safe, and special, then I love you. But when you do not give me love, I feel bad, insecure, and unworthy, then I do not love you. Since you have the power to give or withdraw love (and love is what I want more than anything else), then you must be more powerful than me. I can either submit to this or I can fight it. You are either "for me" or "against me." In other words, you are either my savior or my enemy.* And so the battle begins: a strategy (overt or covert) is employed to get love in the way you want it, according to your story of love. Of course, there are always two people in relationship with two different stories of love, and so there's a mutual power struggle.

This is the how the dream of relationship turns into the drama of relationship. Most people accept or, rather, are resigned to the push and pull of relationship as a normal part of life. Some glamorize it, and call it passion. Others spiritualize it, and call it a dance. Whatever name we choose to call it by, it's actually a war: there is division in you because the other is seen as existing outside of you. And as long as the other is separate from you, they will be the apparent source of either your happiness or your misery. It is impossible to be at peace if your emotional well-being is dependent on someone else. And if you're not at peace, then you're at war with yourself, the other, life, and reality.

In war, there can be no love, because real love has no opposite. Hate is not the opposite of love because real love has no enemy. Real love is complete unto itself. It is not dependent on form, whether this form be your lover, child, dog, the dark chocolate melting in your mouth, the divine artwork on the gallery wall, or your spiritual teacher. Love is your essential nature: it is *in* you, and it really has nothing to do with anyone or anything else. You come to know this (if you are willing to radically open) when that which you most cherish is taken away from you. When you can love without form—in other words, when you stop loving another in order to feel loved and instead simply open to love *as* love—then you are free from the bondage of looking for love.

THE GIFT OF HEARTBREAK WHEN RELATIONSHIP ENDS

The end of something—whether it be the end of a career when you reach retirement age, the end of parenthood when children grow up and leave home, the end of a marriage, love affair, or friendship, or the end of youthfulness when faced with the decline of the physical body—is an invitation to meet the heartbreak of loss. Even the end of a weeklong retreat with a beloved spiritual teacher can leave you feeling bereft when you return to the raw reality of your everyday life. Although it appears that some "thing" in the external world is lost, the end of something is not a material crisis but an existential one. Loss, especially if it is the loss of something we have invested much of ourselves in, brings us to the depths of despair, to a dark and desolate place inside ourselves that is devoid of meaning and purpose. Here, we may experience an excruciating sense of aloneness or abandonment, and it may feel like we can't go on living. But this darkness holds the key to transformation, because in the agony and tragedy of loss, the heart is invited to break.

This heartbreak is a bifurcation point. Just as in any living system that reaches maximum stress, we can either descend into chaos or we can jump into a higher order. Loss brings us to our knees, and at rock bottom the road forks in two. One path leads us into the *story* of loss ("This shouldn't be happening," "Poor me, it's a cruel world," "I don't deserve this," or, "This is the worst thing that has ever happened," and so on), and we get lost in the waves of life's vicissitudes. We either flap around, desperately trying to get to the safety of the other shore, or we sink into depression, alienation, anxiety, and even suicidal thoughts. The other path invites us to dive beneath the waves and surrender to the shoreless ocean, where the depth of suffering becomes a doorway to the discovery of that which cannot ever be lost or gained.

The seemingly unendurable pain of loss, if met all the way, not as the *story* of loss but as the raw, naked experience of *what is*, has the potential to bring us to the devastating edge where the mind cannot go. The willingness that comes from the deepest part of your heart and soul, not from the mind's will-power, to utterly let go of any attempt to manipulate, control, hold onto, or make sense of anything at all, has the capacity to annihilate all false notions of "my security," "my safety," "my stability," and even "my self." Here, in the unfathomable abyss of oceanic consciousness, the story of "me" and "mine" drowns and you fall into an open-ended question that invites you to discover, once and for all, who you really are.

It's a question that asks: "Can your purpose or your life actually be lost? Can love actually be lost? Or is it your role as parent, partner, caretaker, or spiritual teacher that is lost? Is it your plans for the future that are lost? Or perhaps your dream of a perfect, happy, safe, glamorous, or enlightened life is lost?

Are any of these things real; did they ever exist other than as a concept in your mind, as a fantasy of salvation? Or is it *you,* the self-created idea of yourself as *this* or *that,* that is lost? And is this who you really are? Who are you really, without these things, when you are stripped bare of all props, ideas, roles, and identity?"

If you're willing to meet these questions without succumbing to the story of victim, you will inevitably arrive at the core question of spiritual inquiry: "Who am I?" If you're willing to investigate this question—not as an intellectual exercise, but while sitting inside the raw experience of heartbreak—the whole edifice of fabricated identity is likely to come tumbling (or crashing) down. If you hear these words from that part of you that believes itself to exist as a separate "me," this will sound terrifying. But if you listen, *right here and now,* from the silence of your innermost being, you will recognize that this obliteration of the separate self is what you long for. After all, is it not this desire for liberation from the prison of ego that ignited you to set out on the spiritual search? And is it not the incandescent flame of your true nature that keeps pulling you toward the inevitable death of all that is false in you?

To the ego, the end of something is a calamity. The illumination of its sticky identification with form, whether this be physical form such as "my body" and "my relationship," or a psychological form such as "my happiness" and "my love," is a huge threat to its survival. But if your devotion is to waking up out of the dream of ego, the end of something is a great blessing.

The naked moment-to-moment opening to the anguish of heartbreak can offer a more potent spiritual teaching than reading every spiritual book you can get your hands on or chasing every new spiritual teacher in town in the hope that you'll finally arrive at the holy grail of enlightenment. It is life's intelligence that brings loss to your doorstep, not as a punishment, but as a doorway to liberation. It is the fierce face of grace that appears in the guise of tragedy and demands that you awaken out of the dream of separation. It is the reality of love, a radically ruthless love that is unafraid to get its hands dirty in the messy realm of dark emotions, that is calling you back home to itself, so that you come to know yourself *as* love.

The end of a relationship, whether it's divorce, the death of a loved one, or even the death of a beloved pet, is a particularly ruthless teacher. It feels as if your heart is literally breaking in two, as if you and the object of your loss are torn asunder, separated by a huge chasm in time and space, and you are left abandoned, alone, and unloved. In reality, there is no such thing as heartbreak; the heart cannot break, as it is inherently whole and indivisible. But it can *feel* like it's breaking, and this feeling must be met all the way if loss is to be redemptive. What's actually happening when you experience heartbreak is a loosening of self-protective energetic layers that once served to insulate you from hurt and perceived attack (perhaps in your early childhood, teens, and in previous lifetimes) but that now, in *this* moment of your life, function only as a fortress to obscure the luminous openness of your heart.

If you're willing to genuinely ride the torrent of grief that sits inside the feeling of heartbreak, the calcified stories that uphold this relic that no longer serves you will be washed away. Very often, though, there's an avoidance of meeting grief, not only because of the fear of experiencing intense emotions, but also because the mind interprets grief as a story of helplessness. Mostly, the story of helplessness is a part of the bigger story of victimhood, and this becomes a huge barrier to the purification process. As long as you believe yourself to be a victim of circumstance, the mental and emotional contractions are too tightly packed to allow the light of truth to penetrate your heart. However, helplessness can also be the aperture through which you tenderly discover the incandescent majesty of your invulnerable nature by admitting to yourself that you are profoundly helpless in the face of loss. The wholehearted admission of helplessness in the wake of grief is not a weakness but a surrender to the kind of love that detonates all erroneous beliefs in separation and reveals the radiance of your essential nature as wholeness.

If you are experiencing loss in your life right now, or if you have ever experienced loss and are still carrying unmet emotions, are you willing, in *this* moment, to welcome grief as a purifying force? Are you willing to allow all structures of self-protection to be destroyed so that you can discover what is truly indestructible? Are you willing to drown in the waves of seemingly unbearable sadness, rage, regret, despair, and aloneness without clinging to the safety net of any story? Are you ready to discover what remains when everything false in you dies?

When you completely open to grief, without the story of victimhood, the grief passes through you much more quickly. The mind imagines grief to be a kind of purgatory without any light at the end of the tunnel, and sometimes it does indeed seem to be an endless darkness. But, when unconditionally opened to, grief is more like the piercing knife of a surgeon that cuts through the time-bound illusion of woundedness to reveal an eternal ocean of compassion. It's a compassion for yourself, for the one who has gone, and for the unremitting cycle of birth and death that weaves together the experience of life on earth. In this compassion, you are not alone in your heartbreak; loss becomes a universal experience that connects us in the one heart of being.

It is here, in this heart that is broken wide open by loss, that you can discover that the closeness, tenderness, laughter, and tears that were all a part of the relationship are still alive in you. Do you still feel the one who has gone? Do you have an internal dialogue with them? Do the waves of connection, sweetness, joy, and regret still continue? Can you see how the relationship continues in *you*? This intimacy is alive in the present moment as the delicate fragrance of a love that transcends time and space, not as a memory in your mind (although it may include a memory).

Is it possible that the loss of what you have loved has served a more glorious purpose than your mind is willing to accept? Is it possible that what appears to break you in two has actually served to open your heart to the truth of oneness? Can you sense your own inseparability from all that was, all that is, and all that will be?

FEAR OF ALONENESS

If you're radically honest, it's likely, even if you have glimpsed the freedom of a nondual perspective, that you still harbor a deep-seated fear of aloneness. Even though you know the truth of your essential nature as wholeness, maybe you think it would be a bonus to share this truth in a committed relationship. Perhaps you think that living the truth of awakening in everyday life would be easier or more exciting if you could share this life with another who has also awakened. Or maybe you're confused, because although you feel an inner peace, there's still a craving for companionship and security.

Spiritual seekers frequently report that after the light of awakeness has revealed itself, they feel even more disconnected from family, friends, coworkers, and from most of the human population. It's a common experience to wake up out of the dream of separation and feel as if you are the only one who is no longer sleepwalking. This sense of being different from everyone else reveals a deeper aloneness. If this sense of alienation is not explored, it can become a story of spiritual superiority. The story is often one of detachment: "I have transcended the messy realm of human feelings, therefore I am more spiritual." Another common story is disdain: "I have recognized my true nature, but you are all still living in ignorance of your true nature, therefore I am more worthy." Or it may express itself as pity: "I feel sorry for you, I must do something to alleviate your suffering," or "I have arrived at the holy grail of enlightenment, and therefore I am more special." Each of these stories (and any variation on these themes) has ramifications for how you relate to others and how you act in the world. Believing yourself to be more spiritual than others can result in arrogance, aloofness, judgment, and even unkindness: precisely the qualities we do not associate with being spiritual!

Whether the story of spiritual superiority takes the form of detachment, disdain, or an attempt to save the world, it's all a cover-up for the primal fear of abandonment. As newborns, we cannot survive without the close proximity and attention of our mother (or primary caregiver). We need her to feed us, keep us warm, and protect us from harm. This basic physical care is vital. Hopefully, if we are to thrive, our mother will also hold us, touch us, smile at us, and provide us with emotional nourishment. Most living creatures, especially warm-blooded mammals, are totally dependent on their mother in the very early stage of their life. Of course, they soon outgrow this biological necessity and venture into the world with a fearless curiosity and autonomy.

The progression from dependency to independency is a natural pattern of development in humans. But what is essentially a purely biological instinct gets hijacked by the ego and becomes dysfunctional. This hijacking creates a fear of being alone that has nothing to do with the present-moment reality of physical survival; rather, it is about upholding the illusion of "me" as a separate entity. Giving attention to the separate "me" in order to avoid facing the terror of aloneness is very popular. It's an avoidance tactic that comes in many guises. For many people, it is the compulsion to constantly be doing something (for example, "shopping therapy," spring-cleaning the house, reading a magazine, or rolling a cigarette), chasing something (for example, the next big business contract, the attractive waitress at the local restaurant, or the new guru in town), or cultivating connections (for example, social networking or building a portfolio of business clients). For others, it is the obsession with filling up with food, entertainment, technical know-how, or spiritual knowledge. And for some, it is the sense of belonging that comes with joining a like-minded group of people (for example, a football club, a recovery group, or an ethical cause).

All of this, of course, is a part of the rich tapestry of human activity, and there's certainly nothing bad or wrong with any of it. But if you really long for a deep intimacy with life that has nothing to do with how busy, satiated, stimulated, entertained, or connected you are, but is totally fulfilling unto itself, then all avoidance tactics must be exposed. The refusal to tell the truth of the horror of your aloneness sidetracks the possibility of fully waking up out of the dream of separation. When the black hole of aloneness is avoided, it becomes a story of loneliness. You can be surrounded by a thousand people dancing at a party or a hundred people sitting silently at a spiritual retreat, you can gather with twenty friends to celebrate your birthday or three friends for an intimate evening meal, you can even be making love with your partner in a committed relationship, and still be lonely.

Loneliness expresses itself in many ways. It can be a nagging sense of disconnection, a pervading shyness, an acute sense of alienation, an inability to be still or silent, or it can manifest as a deep depression. In a smaller percentage of people, loneliness is so all-consuming that there is a severe withdrawal from everyday interactions. This is what we call "the lone wolf" or "the recluse," and in more extreme cases, "the misanthropist."

Whichever way loneliness expresses itself, it's a barren landscape, with seemingly no way out. And there is a truth here: there *is* no way out. In order to go beyond loneliness, you must go *through* it. You must walk through the valley of desolation. The story of loneliness ("I'm all alone," "Nobody loves me," "There's no one here for me," "I am rejected/abandoned," "I am an outcast") cannot be leisurely cast aside. Full attention must be given, first and foremost, to the exposure of loneliness by telling the truth (to yourself) of the black hole of emptiness you experience. After exposure, it then must be met *all* the way if the darkness is to be genuinely transformed. This means getting right up close and intimate, not with the story, but with the naked experience of loneliness. Of course, this is scary, because it seems that if you surrender to the desolate darkness of loneliness, you will die. And yes, the you that believes itself to exist as a separate entity *will* die. It's actually the *idea* of you as a separate entity, the story of "me" that dies, not the real you. But it *feels* like the real you will die, and the horror of this imagined possibility must be faced. No words of explanation or reassurance, not even the words offered on this page, can cushion the undisguised fear that arises on this inward journey. You must discover for yourself what is true.

To transform the desolate story of loneliness into the truth of what lies inside the story requires you to go very deep and to open very wide. It's a request for communion. Communion is more than a connection or meeting with someone or with something. It's an immeasurable embrace in which all residue of separation evaporates. In order to commune, whether it be with your lover, your beloved cat, the grand old oak tree in the park, the night sky, or with God, there must be no labeling of your experience ("my loneliness," "my misery," or "my tragedy"). There must be no categorizing as better or worse than what was and what might be, or as more or less than anyone else's experience.

Loneliness is an invitation to deeply relax, to commune with that which you have spent a lifetime trying to cover over with mental and emotional contortions. It's an invitation to sit inside the desolation without flinching or tightening and to allow the darkness to embrace you. And even though it may seem that this darkness is something outside of you, something you can *choose to sit inside,* it is, in fact, sitting *inside you.* It *is* you as the primordial void of beingness that exists prior to your birth into form. Relaxation means you fall into this void. And, in doing so, you fall in love with yourself.

FALLING IN LOVE WITH YOURSELF

The "self-love" that's mostly talked about in today's culture of self-empowerment and pop psychology refers to doing things that are pleasurable to you, such as pampering your body, buying yourself nice "treats," hanging out with friends, thinking only positive thoughts about yourself, and so on. What I'm referring to as self-love is much more revolutionary than any of this. It's revolutionary because it has the power to evolve you beyond ego, once and for all.

I'm pointing to a love that resides in the unrestrained dimension of being, not in the constrains of your mind, nor even within the boundaries of your heart. It's an inexhaustible communion, an infinitely intimate situation. How can anything be more intimate than meeting your deepest, most innermost being? In this intimacy, subject and object, observer and observed, inside and outside, "me" and "you" all vanish. What remains is not a desolate emptiness (as the ego likes to imagine), but a shimmering fullness that includes everything and yet is not defined by its contents. We could call this an "empty fullness" or a "full emptiness"; either way, words are insufficient in encapsulating the unmistakable experience of this. It is the experience of all-one-ness, which is another way of saying aloneness.

Aloneness *is* your true nature. You are, in fact, absolutely alone every moment of your life. You may be holding hands with your lover, playing with your children, jostling through crowds in the city streets, or dancing with a thousand other sweaty bodies, but your experience cannot be shared with anyone else. It can only be experienced through *your* body-mind vehicle. We are each born absolutely alone, even though we are still connected to our mother. And we each die absolutely alone, even if we are surrounded by our loved ones. We may try to deny or avoid this seemingly stark reality by stubbornly clinging to handed-down beliefs (perhaps about an afterlife, reincarnation, or the eternal soul) or by refusing to even acknowledge death as a part of life, but it actually cannot be any other way. To expose this raw truth and to completely give yourself over to it creates an inner marriage or alchemical process in which the devastation of death gives birth to the elixir of immutable silence.

In the unfathomable silence of being, which is the same as saying "aloneness," all concepts of self-love are utterly without substance. Just as with falling in love with another, falling into the abyss of aloneness brings an end to all seeking. As you stop trying to hold on to anything at all, there is a profound relaxation into your intrinsic nature as wholeness. The fictitious "self" as a separate entity dies and the real self is realized *as* love.

While the dream of finding wholeness through another now finally comes to an end, the emanation of love *through* you and *as* you is unstoppable. As this love comes to be embodied as an everyday living reality, it can't help but overflow into your environment: everything is touched by this and is transformed to a higher order. But before we go on to explore how this love gives birth to a whole new paradigm of relationship, our conversation needs to turn (briefly) to an exploration of another big myth—that spirituality and relationship are not good bedfellows.

CHAPTER 8

Love and Enlightened Relationship

SPIRITUALITY AS AN EXCUSE TO AVOID INTIMACY

Most traditional spiritual teachings consider relationship to be a distraction from the purity of the spiritual path. While it is true that the addictive cycle of looking for wholeness through another is an obstacle to enlightenment, when this truth is interpreted by the unenlightened mind it sets up an even bigger obstacle. The desire to transcend the messy and painful world of emotions and intimate human relationship is a major stumbling block for many seekers. Very often, it's the desire to find freedom from this pain that sets off the spiritual search in the first place. But the spiritual search itself can easily become an avoidance tactic. This is convenient, since it is in alignment with a nondual perspective that insists on the absolute realm of pristine emptiness and invalidates the relative realm of the manifest. After all, if the world is an illusion, and if "you" and "me" do not exist, then surely relationship is meaningless, and do I really need to get involved in the mess of it all?

While saying that "only consciousness is real" sounds very enlightened, it's frequently a cover-up for the raw fact that the human experience hurts. The refusal to open to this hurt is the very thing that prolongs a deeper suffering. When the horror, agony, and tragedy of the human experience remains unacknowledged, it goes underground and becomes lodged in the psyche as a sense of meaninglessness, alienation, and even nihilism. In the body, it can manifest as tightness or ungroundedness. Of course, the person in whom all this is manifesting is usually totally (or at least partially) unaware of any of it. If what you truly desire is authentic freedom, this cover-up must be exposed. But this very exposure can be painful. It breaks the heart open to admit that you are afraid to open to what may hurt. It's like trying to turn the key in an old lock that's become encrusted with dust and rust, over many years of neglect. It just doesn't want to budge and requires considerable effort to overcome the resistance.

This exposure demands your willingness to be fully intimate with the totality of life's phenomenal display. Everything is in relationship to everything else: *you* are in perpetual relationship to the world. Whether you believe the world is an illusion or not does not matter, because beliefs do not negate the fact that you are having an earthly experience. Authentic freedom requires you to consciously surrender all lopsided notions of "only consciousness is real" and to meet, with innocent openness, the naked reality of your experience.

THE TRUE PURPOSE OF RELATIONSHIP

Denial or avoidance of any experience at all, whether it is an earthly experience or a spiritual one, limits your perception and cannot possibly reveal the unbounded vista of truth. Any attempt to use spirituality as an excuse to avoid intimacy perpetuates the inherited war between human and divine, passed down by millennia of religious and scientific conditioning.

The invitation offered in the pages of this book is for you to put aside the archaic idea of enlightenment as a renunciation of the world and to be a pioneer of a new conversation in spirituality. Will you join the increasing number of spiritual seekers for whom this idea of renunciation no longer rings true? Will you join the increasing number of people who are now asking new, far-reaching questions that extend across the apparent divide between consciousness and the world to embrace the crazy paradox of being *in* the world but not *of* it? Relationship is perhaps the place where these questions are the most urgent, for while it appears that relationship is a very personal (and even a very selfish) matter, it actually has much more to do with the transformation of the world than it does about you.

Why? Because it's in the furnace of intimacy that the collective shadow, which plays itself out as greed, corruption, and destruction, is illuminated and transmuted to compassion. Every time you turn away from or deny what is here in *your* experience, you add to the darkness in the world because you are divided within. Every time you deeply accept or open to what is here, you set the world alight because you are radiant with an inner oneness. You are the cause of war and peace in the world, because the world is inseparable from who you are as consciousness. And right in the midst of the messiness of relationship is where war can stop and peace can begin. Because it's when we're at our most vulnerable that we either fall back into ego by implementing the age-old strategy of defense and attack, or we rise into a new way of being by recognizing that we are all intimately connected and that each of us is an expression of one beingness.

Relationship can offer the possibility of an enlightened humanity, because in every interaction it has the capacity to return us to the wholeness of love. If you are willing to open to this possibility of allowing relationship to be your spiritual practice, then relationship will evolve out of the dream (and the drama) to serve its true purpose of transforming the world.

RELATIONSHIP AS SPIRITUAL PRACTICE

Relationship is a potent medicine. It invites you to get right up close and intimate with everything that is unilluminated in you. Every ugly emotion and dark feeling that has been pushed away because you've deemed them unacceptable becomes unimaginably highlighted in the torchlight of intimacy. The messy arena of relationship, where two individuals each want their needs met, to be understood, to be heard, and to be loved, is the testing ground where our buttons get pushed and we involuntarily send off missiles to destroy our enemy or erect impenetrable walls of defense. This ancient mechanism of attack and defense is a very effective strategy for avoiding an honest meeting with the raw energy beneath the reactivity. It's raw because it's the hurt and vulnerability that was not met when the abuse or rejection first happened, and you were too small and powerless to face it. If this past trauma has not been consciously processed and integrated into your psyche, it remains in the shadows of your subconscious, waiting for the opportunity to be seen and fully held in the heart of acceptance.

Trigger points are not a sign that something is terribly wrong, but a sign of love's intelligence calling everything back home to itself. It's a return to healing and wholeness. Love, disguised as a trigger, is an unrelenting invitation for you to open *now*. Whatever happened in the past, it does not matter *now*. Whatever your story of victimhood or wounding, it does not matter *now*. What matters now is your willingness to open to the raw energy that is *here*, to be vulnerable to the unfoldment of this unfiltered moment and all that it offers ... *all* of it, not just the bits you like. The invitation is to stop filtering reality through your "likes" and "dislikes," to stop following the horizontal movement of the egoic mind as it takes a snapshot of now and compares it with the past, and to radically and irrevocably stop labeling this moment as "unbearable" or "the worst thing that ever happened to me." Just stop *right here* and be fully, wholeheartedly, and lovingly with what *is*.

Your unconditional acceptance of what is here is the resolution of all that is fragmented in you. It's the remedy for all that is sick in the world. The root of judgment and the resulting resentment, rejection, hostility, and hatred lies in your lack of acceptance of that which you believe to be bad or wrong in *you*. If you're on a spiritual path (which undoubtedly you are, if you're reading this book), then the root of judgment lies in your lack of acceptance of all that is unspiritual or unenlightened in you. The one who triggers you the most is your best friend, because relationship is a powerful mirror and always reflects back to you that which you don't accept in yourself—so that you *see* it and choose to befriend it. The one you hate the most is your greatest spiritual teacher, because *right here,* in the dark cloud of your righteousness, rage, and revulsion, is the radical opportunity for you to stop doing what you've automatically done for a lifetime or more, and instead choose to open to what is *beneath* your reactivity. This opening allows the rawness of terror and horror to melt into the tenderness of vulnerability and grief. It's a breaking open of the heart to welcome everything back home to rest in love.

Perhaps you can now see that the spiritual bypassing of the messy world of relationship is no longer an intelligent option if we are to be harbingers of peace in the world, today and beyond. The deeper purpose of relationship is to be a catalyst for spiritual evolution, for your own sake and for the sake of humanity. It's in the midst of the hurt and raging emotion that we can become conscious of where we are divided within. The reason there is more turbulence in relationship, as well as more urgency to find the perfect relationship than ever before, is because relationship is an evolutionary driver and we are being offered a powerful opportunity to bring light to darkness in the messiness of our everyday lives.

Are you willing here and *now* to take up this invitation? Are you willing to be the portal through which light can enter the world? It's a potent invitation ... are you willing to say *yes?* You don't have to be concerned about finding a relationship. If you are honestly willing to open your heart and let love in, despite the high possibility of "unacceptable" and "unspiritual" feelings, relationship will find you at the right time. You do not need to do anything to make this happen; life's intelligence will inevitably offer this opportunity.

MEETING EACH OTHER IN OPENNESS

There are countless books telling us how to have a perfect relationship. We're told what to say, what to do, what to think, and what to feel in order to have maximum passion, satisfaction, and commitment. If we're experiencing conflict, such as escalating arguments, unexpected outbursts of tears, or a stony silence, we have access to a vast array of methods to help us mend or improve relationship, including marriage counseling, effective communication training, life coaching, couples therapy, family therapy, and sex therapy. Even in spiritual circles it's fashionable to turn to tantra to learn techniques for achieving an ecstatic union that promises more happiness, bliss, and love.

While all these methods can be a useful support system, there's a danger of missing the mark. The attempt to mend, improve, or even spiritualize relationship, when rooted in need, has no possibility of real transformation. "Need" is the same as saying "codependency." If you are spiritual, this term is likely to be abhorrent to you, because codependency is commonly equated with neurotic dysfunction. But codependency is the state of the majority of relationships. Unless you have irrevocably fallen in love with aloneness, need will be the main operating system. Even the tendency in spiritual circles to use relationship as a "path to higher consciousness" is based in need. This may be challenging to hear, as there is often a big investment in this belief, but I invite you to tenderly hear these words, not from your mind but from a deep, quiet space within yourself. I invite you to consider that as long as there is even a whisper of need, there is an inevitable fear of loss and an accompanying strategy to prevent this loss.

Some of the most common hidden agendas within code-pendent relationship run like this: "I need you to love me according to my image of love, otherwise I'll withdraw my love," "I need you to be successful/beautiful/spiritual/happy, otherwise I can't love you completely," "I need you to be my perfect partner/my best friend/my soul mate/the one for me, otherwise I can't feel complete," and so on. I invite you to expose these agendas. Do you need your partner to do or to be something, according to your picture of a perfect relationship? Do you need your partner to have the same viewpoints and opinions as you, to like doing the same activities as you, to tell you that you're beautiful/sexy/clever/strong/perfect, to always agree with you, to do anything to please you/make you happy? Do you need your mother/father/sister/brother to give you lots of attention, to listen to you, to recognize your star-quality, to have the same values or spiritual beliefs as you? Do you need your spiritual teacher to be kind to you, to be gentle, to always listen, to never show disapproval or irritation with you, to treat you as "special"? I invite you to be ruthlessly honest here. Are any of these questions (or any variation of them) true for you?

There's really nothing wrong with any of this. Need is a part of the human experience, especially when there has not been enough loving care and support in our early years. What's important here is that you tell the truth to yourself, that you dig deeper than any self-judgment you may have, that you shine a light on any mental and emotional acrobatics that hide the raw truth of your needs. Very often, this exposure is more challenging than it appears, because admitting to our needs is an admission of vulnerability. The deeper we go into the tender truth of our heart, the closer we get to the core wound of separation. But it's in our open vulnerability that we can discover that which is eternally free and always whole.

The true gift of relationship is its capacity to correct the erroneous belief that you need anyone or anything to fulfill you. The good news is that you do not need to live a monastic life of seclusion and celibacy in order to purify yourself of need. While consciously choosing to withdraw from intimate relationship is sometimes a useful support in the process of clearing codependent patterns, intimate relationship itself has the power to transform the multi-cloaked burden of need into a naked openness that allows a whole new dimension of relationship to be revealed. It means you do not need to pretend or perform acrobatics in order to please your partner or to keep a picture of the "perfect relationship" intact. It means you stand together at the edge of the unknown, willing to explore and delve into the difficult feelings and moments even though it is incredibly scary and it hurts. Here, at this unendingly new edge, there is no manipulation, exploitation, or coercion; there is just an open space of inquiry where we can discover what is true.

THE DIRECT PATH OF NAKED TRUTH

The willingness to discover what is true in the midst of conflict, hurt, disappointment, or disconnection is the direct path in relationships. There is no need to learn special techniques or communication skills, or to practice visualization or rituals. There is no magic or mystery in the direct path other than the wonder and mystery of love itself.

This is about simply telling the truth without cloaking, decorating, embellishing, blaming, judging, or defending. It's actually not about the other, but about what is true in *you*. Telling the naked truth requires you to meet what is here in the unknownness of *this* moment. It's not a preplanned speech or testimony, but rather an innocent openness that leads to a radical honesty in which you stay present without wavering into past hurt or future expectation. It's also about being willing to listen to the truth without protecting yourself, rejecting the other, blaming, judging, or defending. It requires you to stay tenderly yet unequivocally open in the midst of confusion, brokenness, or anger, and to renounce all need to cling to relationship or to discard relationship.

In this open space of self-exposure, the desire to control anyone or anything simply stops, and so does the search for something other than what is in the present moment. Without a story to stick to and without a "me" burdened by agenda or self-protective strategy, everything that stands in the way of openness (every complaint, doubt, regret, and resentment) tenderly reveals itself and returns to source. In this pregnant moment of stillness, there is absolutely nothing you need to plan, consider, or do. The next moment simply and irrevocably reveals itself in the ever-unfolding moment of what is true. Whether you stay in the relationship or leave the relationship, whether you cry or laugh with joy, feel agony or ecstasy, all unfolds according to life's intelligence. In the openness of stark naked truth, whether you like what you are experiencing or not, there is only the deepest acceptance.

In going beyond codependency and meeting each other in the deepest acceptance, the other stops being defined by their role and you stop being defined by your role. This is the end of the dream (and the end of the nightmare) of relationship, and the beginning of the reality of relating. It's as if a worn-out edifice, weighed down by millennia of dogma, tradition, stereotypes, rules, and misunderstandings, finally comes tumbling down to clear the way for new growth.

Relating means you are free of the burden of trying to uphold a special relationship. The war has ended because there are no longer two separate individuals (or two cultures or two nations) battling to get their needs met. Instead, this new dimension of openly relating where you tell the truth and listen to the truth offers you the radical and enlightening possibility of recognizing that there is only one consciousness expressing itself through everything. Instead of taking up a posture of either domination or submission, you are now free to mutually bow down to the sacredness of truth in all things and in all circumstances.

Relating is the seed that gives birth to an authentically awakened or enlightened relationship. This kind of relationship, while very natural, is like a delicate flower that's only just beginning to peek through the crack in the concrete. It's a rare occurrence. It's rare because millennia of social, cultural, and religious conditioning around gender roles has covered over the purity of real love. As consciousness awakens to itself through the vehicle of humanity, this is likely to change.

FROM CONSCIOUS RELATIONSHIP TO ENLIGHTENED RELATIONSHIP

Enlightened relationship is often confused with conscious relationship, but there's a fundamental difference, and it is helpful to untangle any confusion about the differences between them. In conscious relationship, there are two individuals practicing "being conscious." This may take many forms of expression, which is usually about sharing values of personal and planetary awareness, such as living a "green" lifestyle, being involved in ecological or humanitarian projects, setting up an ethical or holistic business, conscious parenting, finding ways to express creativity, and developing a positive attitude. If it's also a "spiritual relationship," it may include a shared goal of achieving enlightenment, following the same teacher, traveling to spiritual places together, praying to the same spiritual deity, or dedicating a significant portion of time to tantric practices or meditation.

While all of this is a wonderful movement toward being conscious in relationship, if the emphasis is on the outer form, however ethically, ecologically, or spiritually conscious it may be, there cannot be a flowering into real love. Instead, the relationship becomes a way to strengthen the ego's identification with a separate self, because shared values become the scaffolding that upholds a sense of being right, good, worthy, or spiritual. If you and your partner agree about these values (and the actions and activities that are a product of these values), you feel safe and loved, and there is calm and happiness in the relationship. But if these values change or you disagree, love can quickly turn to resentment, rejection, judgment, and hate.

There is often a hidden code of conduct in ethically, ecologically, and spiritually conscious relationship, and unspoken rules about how to think, feel, speak, and act. With this comes an expectation (usually unconscious) that the other will adhere to these rules, otherwise they will not be the "conscious partner" you need. As long as there is an agenda, however subtle, and however "for the good of the relationship" it is, there will be a strategy (either overt or covert) to avoid loss of a partner, security, comfort, or cherished "conscious beliefs."

This is more positive than a codependent relationship, but is nevertheless just as entangled.

However, if there is a genuine desire to go beyond unconscious egoic patterns, and a sincere commitment to truth, this kind of relationship is a powerful doorway for spiritual growth: it is so much closer to the possibility of a paradigm shift than the heavily role-based relationships of previous generations. The invitation of this relationship then becomes one of sacrificing all expectation, agenda, strategy, and all cherished notions of conscious or spiritual relationship. If you really want to be conscious in relationship, the invitation is for you to stop being concerned with whether your partner is conscious or spiritual (according to your image of what this looks like), and take responsibility for your own state of consciousness.

If the light of consciousness is strong in you, and you are willing to be unwaveringly present and unconditionally open in the midst of disagreement or disappointment, the other is unlikely to remain unconscious for long. They will rise up to meet you in consciousness, and with time the undeniable fragrance of real love will permeate the relationship. Or they will be triggered into reactivity and fall back down to further unconsciousness, in which case you will be challenged to not follow them into unconsciousness. Or the relationship will end, and in this ending you are offered an opportunity for a profound transformation.

If you are present and open during the end of relationship, when sadness, regret, doubt, confusion, and fear threaten to engulf you, and the other is angry, resentful, rejected, or helpless, you are likely to move into an inner dimension of the unconditional heart. In this place there is the recognition that the relationship may end but that love never ends. Love cannot leave you, because it is indivisible from your true nature, and so it will continue to flow through your life. This may be through another partner who is able to meet you in truth, a friendship or family relationship that is renewed by your tender openness, or a spiritual teacher that reflects the clarity of your inner radiance. Or it may be through a creative project or a humanitarian cause that you devote yourself to, or simply through your heart as an ineffable joy that becomes the backdrop to your life. If you remain utterly conscious within this inner dimension, you are likely to recognize your true self *as* love.

When your true self is realized *and* embodied as love, the need to find wholeness through another totally falls away. When every cell of your being has remembered itself as the essential wholeness of love, the totality of existence fulfills you. With nothing more to gain, acquire, or look for, everything comes to rest in a deep silence that it totally fulfilled. Forms (a person, an animal, a project, or a work of art) continue to appear in your life, because it is the nature of form to appear and disappear. This is the play of existence, yet all forms that appear in your experience are innately recognized as arising out of, and returning to, the silence of being. If someone appears in your life, and they too have recognized and embodied (or at least are on the journey of embodiment) a deeper dimension of being, a new paradigm is born: an enlightened and authentically awakened relationship.

WHEN THE SILENCE IN YOU MEETS THE SILENCE IN ANOTHER

Enlightened relationship is what happens when the silence in you meets the silence in another. When each individual has totally fallen in love with aloneness and fully embodies their own wholeness, it's no longer about mutual satisfaction, pleasure, comfort, or security, nor about feeling loved and wanted. Without dependency, there is no longer an attempt to change or fix or please the other. Nor is there any attempt to agree (or disagree). It's not a battle of opinions, because there is neither an enemy nor a victim, and neither is there an attempt to spiritualize the relationship. There's really no need to practice any spiritual method or even "be conscious," because it's not something you can make happen by doing something, nor is it something you can understand intellectually. It doesn't have anything to do with following the right spiritual teacher or the right spiritual teaching. Enlightened relationship blossoms only in the deepest silence, when all false constructs of separation are destroyed, and there is only the unadulterated recognition of emptiness dancing through duality. Only here can true love flourish.

True love meets the essence of love in all people and all things. It's not reserved just for "the one." You could say it's an impersonal (or universal) love, but this does not mean the human bond with your partner, if you're in relationship, is any less vibrant. It means you are not dependent on anything outside of you to give you love or to make you feel loved or to make you feel loving, and neither do you try to possess or hoard the love. Instead, you are simply the open space through which love flows, because real love simply can't help but move through any vehicle that is empty of the residue of conditional love. This love has nothing to do with being nice or acting in any particular way. It's an invisible emanation of light that gently touches all that is unilluminated in its vicinity and has the power to transform. There will be those who are repelled by this because they resist transformation. And there will be those who are magnetically drawn to this because they are ripe for an inner revolution of consciousness.

The two individuals in an enlightened relationship are not aware that anything special is happening, because just like enlightenment itself, enlightened relationship is actually extraordinarily ordinary! It only becomes special, holy, or mystical when the ego takes ownership of it, and then it is not an authentically enlightened relationship, but a facsimile of this. Just as with enlightenment, there are actually no rules about what an enlightened relationship looks like in its outer form. It's the inner dimension that matters, and here there is only the sense that there is no more "relationship." In other words, there are no longer two individuals *having* a relationship; instead there is one beingness shimmering through all forms and through the space within which all forms appear. This is not an intellectual realization, but an almost palpable experience that flickers in and out of everyday perception and yet is unmistakably present in all things.

You may have already glimpsed this open space of beingness, but perhaps you have not recognized it as love or even been conscious of it. You'll experience this space in moments of stillness as you watch the sun majestically rise over the horizon, when the melody of a bird's song makes you silent inside, or when the beauty of the mountain peaks catches your breath. You'll also experience this space when you stop and look into the eyes of your child, when you're lost in dancing, or when you savor that first sip of tea. It's right here *now*, in the gap between thoughts, in the pause between the in-breath and out-breath, and in the space between these words.

BEYOND SEX

I am often asked about what happens to sexual attraction in an enlightened relationship. While the conversation about sex has been totally avoided in most traditional spiritual teachings (and in many modern-day spiritual circles), this is a question that is now being asked more frequently as more people awaken.

The question of what happens to sex in an authentically awakened relationship needs to be truthfully investigated within your own direct experience, as there is no "right way." The real inquiry is not about what happens on the surface but about discovering what is beneath the social, cultural, and gender-based push and pull (and beneath the biological pull) of the sexual impulse. Regardless of your gender, or whether you're in an opposite-sex or same-sex relationship, the conversation about awakening and sex is really about the purification of gender stereotypes. It's about releasing archaic contractions that uphold any inherited images and behaviors of what it means to be a man or a woman. In awakened sexual relations, you come to rest in a deep inner unity that encompasses both polarities of masculine and feminine and yet transcends both.

Each of us, including every living thing in nature, holds both masculine and feminine energies within. Think of a tree that stands strong in the face of a storm and yet yields to the movement of the wind; it is both fully rooted as itself in the masculine quality of presence, and fully open to the flow of life as the feminine quality of receptivity. Or think of a cat that chases a mouse; it is single-minded in its pursuit (an active or masculine quality, also called the *yang* principle of nature), and yet totally relaxed if the chase comes to nothing (a passive or feminine quality, also called the *yin* principle of nature).

Of course, at the deepest level, there really is no masculine or feminine. Life does not divide itself in this way. What we call masculine and feminine are inseparable aspects of wholeness. You come to know this when you have authentically awakened to and embodied your true nature as wholeness. When masculine and feminine are in harmony within, there is no longer a polarity. One principle is not in opposition to the other. There is no push and pull. There is only the simplicity of beingness shining through every action and nonaction; there is a oneness with the expression of life.

But for the vast majority of people, whether they are in an opposite-sex or same-sex relationship, there is a strong masculine-feminine polarity; what we often refer to as "sexual chemistry." The stronger the polarity, the more sexual attraction there is, and the more tension, conflict, or passion. The purpose of sex (beyond reproduction) is to heal the division between masculine and feminine. It's what happens at the point of orgasm when, for a moment, the separate self dissolves and you experience a glimpse of freedom. In this moment you feel an inner completeness and there's a sense of harmony with your partner. But, of course, this is a temporary fix and needs to be repeated. This is the addictive cycle of sex, which is often mistaken for love. The allure of this addiction is enough to keep a relationship intact, but not always happy. Sometimes the tension or conflict needs to be transformed consciously, perhaps through couples therapy or tantric practices, and this may be sufficient to keep both partners in the relationship satisfied and even happy. But there's a whole new dimension of love that becomes available when the dynamic of sexual polarity no longer is the primary engine of relationship.

Perhaps you are now wondering what happens to passion and pleasure. Or you are concerned that the relationship will become dry or boring. But it's definitely not about suppressing sexual desire or becoming celibate because of some spiritual ideal. All aspects of sexuality must first be fully allowed. All vestiges of shame, guilt, repression, and perversion must be purified by being consciously present within your sexual expression. (This is not about indulgence, nor violation of boundaries, but about noncensorship within an openly consensual dynamic.) The invitation is for you to discover for yourself what happens when you move from inner stillness to the energetic flow. It's a delicate discovery, one that requires a tender self-honesty and openness to all possible outcomes.

In whichever way it is expressed, sex is always an invitation to be consciously present amid irrepressible surges of energy. Sex becomes spiritual practice if it takes you deeper into presence. When presence is your natural state and oneness is realized as your true nature, it is very likely that there's nothing more to gain by seeking oneness through sex. It's at this point that the ancient compulsion of sexual attraction naturally falls away. Of course, because sexual energy is so linked to the biological impulse of procreation, as well as to a psychological sense of power or aliveness, there may be a lingering resistance to this natural process of growth. But if you are willing to surrender all notions of *should* and *shouldn't*, all subtle clinging to your identity as masculine or feminine, and all cherished ideas of love and relationship, you will see that this is not a loss but a rebirth. It's like shedding old skin; you simply grow out of it.

What remains is a great tenderness that neither refuses physical intimacy nor involves sexual tension or compulsion. In other words, sex becomes much more than a physical exchange between two individuals (although it may include it; there are no rules). Instead, there is an intimate communion with the totality of life, in which every interaction, touch, word, breath, and moment of your experience is a divine union. This includes ordinary moments, such as tending the flowers in the garden or walking the dog. It's at this point that the mesmerizing but potentially exhausting push and pull of gender-based expression comes to rest, and out of the silence of being, a unified melody of an unconditioned heart emerges.

When relationship stops being about pleasure, comfort, or reproduction (although it can, of course, include the act of consciously birthing a child), there's a transmutation of sexual energy that gives birth to something that serves the world. This may be outwardly expressed as a creative project, an innovative social enterprise, or a philanthropic business that touches the lives of many around the globe. Or it may be a quieter expression, with no obvious outer manifestation, but with a heart of gold that touches those close by. Either way, there is no personal investment, agenda, or ownership, just an honest response to the way life wants to move through you *as* you. It's very likely that this transmutation of sexual energy happens in a relationship that has matured, perhaps over several years, when the initial fire of passion becomes a gentle glow, although in some relationships it may happen very early on (remember, there are no rules). This has nothing to do with lack of intimacy; on the contrary, this is the activation of a luminous love that never ends.

But do not take what is written here as gospel truth. Once again, I invite you to discover for yourself what is true for *you* and be willing to surrender everything, including your cherished beliefs about what *should* and *shouldn't* happen in relationship, to a love that is beyond imagination. You cannot package this love and keep it for yourself, nor claim it as a trophy to remind you when it fades, but you *can* know it as that which is without limits or constraints.

CHAPTER 9

The Body as A Gateway
To Liberation

THE ERROR OF IGNORING THE BODY
IN SPIRITUAL INQUIRY

Another very intimate relationship we need to pay attention to is the one we have with our bodies. What happens when we awaken out of the dream of identification with form and yet still appear to function in an earthly body? How do we make sense of knowing ourselves as the eternal presence of consciousness while also knowing that our lives are finite? And does any of this have an impact on how we live?

Many spiritual seekers and spiritual teachers dismiss the body as an inconvenient illusion, and this has led to a lot of confusion. For thousands of years, spiritual teachings have pointed to the absolute purity and perfection of the unmanifest realm of consciousness, while mostly ignoring any conversation about the role of the body in living the truth of consciousness in everyday life. What little attention has been given to the body has mostly emphasized the unlawfulness of our animal nature. In both Eastern and Western spiritual traditions, a plethora of ascetic and punitive practices have developed to conceal or control our natural instincts: celibacy, long periods of fasting, seclusion, abstinence from intimate relationships and worldly interactions, extreme yogic postures, exposing the body to freezing temperatures, and mortification of the flesh have all been attempted throughout history. Some metaphysical and New Age teachings support this disembodied view of spirituality by focusing on out-of-body experiences, trance states, channeling spiritual entities, and communication with angels as ways to achieve a "higher consciousness," but none of these methods has ever led to enlightenment.

The myth of the body as flawed or sinful adds fuel to the suppression of the earth-based feminine that honors all expressions as sacred, including the natural instincts of the body. Not only has this caused rampant havoc and suffering for millions of women across cultures throughout history (and still does in many parts of the world), but this violence toward our holistic nature has filtered into modern-day spiritual circles, where it perpetuates a subtle but no less harmful psychological suffering.

Strictly nondual beliefs such as "The body is an illusion," "Only consciousness is real," and "I am not my body," are very often a convenient excuse for avoiding an awkward and potentially painful inquiry that challenges the much-cherished notion of awakening as a transcendent state without the messiness of the human experience. If this becomes a spiritually rigid perspective, the full maturation of awakening cannot take place. I have met many spiritual seekers who have undeniably experienced the truth of nondual awareness and yet clearly exhibit signs of dissociation. An inability to maintain eye contact, sit still for long periods of time, being out of touch with feelings, difficulty in experiencing intimacy, a sense of viewing life from a distance, and a tendency to experience panic attacks are all common and indicate that the light of awakeness has not yet descended from mind to heart and belly. It's in the tender recesses of the heart and in the cellular memory of the body that unwelcome energies from the past coalesce into the intensity of dark emotions and unresolved trauma. Most often this manifests as a physical armoring (experienced as tension, tightness, and tiredness) and a physiological overreactivity (experienced as emotional numbness combined with emotional outbursts). If awakeness is to flow into our everyday lives, all these contractions must be fully opened to as a feeling-sense.

However much the body is seen to be an illusion, the very real suffering of pain and loss on a human level is unavoidable. If addictions and unwholesome lifestyle behaviors are not examined, they are likely to lead to a decline in physical activity and the manifestation of unremitting pain and disease. Even if there is no obvious physical disease, the natural course of aging and eventually death will have to be faced. The body may well be an inconvenience, but it's a persistent inconvenience!

Are you willing to meet the inconvenient truth of your body? Perhaps there is a fear in the back of your mind that if you fully embrace the reality of your physical experience, the rarified stillness of nondual awareness will be tainted, you'll fall from the giddy heights of transcendence into the density of the human experience, and you'll forget who you really are as consciousness and descend into egoic suffering. Or maybe you are willing to see that you are already suffering if you remain attached to a transcendent viewpoint. Are you willing to examine the fear of facing the agony of what has been locked into your body for a lifetime? Are you willing to face the horror of loss as the body disintegrates when pain, illness, and eventually death arrive on your doorstep? And are you willing to surrender all your notions of what it looks like and feels like to be awakened?

If your answer is a resounding *yes*, then the possibility of discovering what is truly alive and free inside every manifestation, however agonizing or terrifying, is very close. By being unafraid to get up close and intimate with the earthly reality of your body and with every part of your earthly life, an awakened awareness gets polished into the jewel of awakened living.

DISCOVERING THE LUMINOSITY OF BEING PRESENT IN THE BODY

Contrary to what the egoic mind may like to believe, liberation from the suffering of pain and loss associated with physical form comes not by escaping the body, but by being fully present *in* the body. When illness, an accident, or the decline of the body with age show up, the vast majority of people are lost in the story of "poor me." With personal ownership of physical form ("my body"), and with the psychological forms inevitably wrapped around this primary identity ("my pain," "my sickness," "my imperfection," "my ugliness," "my weakness," "my loss," and so on), a story gets created called "my suffering." This fixation on form paradoxically indicates a lack of presence in the body or, rather, in the deeper energy field of the body.

Unlike most people, animals are fully present in their bodies and yet do not suffer. It's obvious that they do experience discomfort and pain, but it's unlikely that they experience psychological suffering. If you have ever lived with a cat, spent time with a dog, or watched the pigeons in the park, you're likely to have sensed how even if they are sick, maimed, or exhausted, there is no drama of "poor me." Of course, we cannot absolutely know what they are experiencing, but we can know that without the capacity for self-reflection— that is, without an ego—there cannot be a separate "me" that identifies with physical form, and there can be no personal ownership of the experience. Without a story of suffering, there is simply and innocently a seamless and fluctuating, unnamed and unowned energy experience. If you are quietly present with any animal in pain or dying (unless there is severe injury that causes the nervous system to react with convulsions), you'll sense the stillness and silence within which this animal is resting; in other words, it is simply *being*.

Of course, that's not to say we shouldn't mend a broken bone, sew up a wound, tend to our bruises, or even rub nourishing oils into our skin. All of this, and more, has its place in the care and maintenance of physical life-forms. But without diving deeper into the ocean of beingness, we remain swimming on the surface, trying to catch and perfect each wave according to our image of how it should be, and there is no lasting fulfillment or real healing in this.

It's the willingness to turn within, to be unequivocally present with every sensation and every feeling, that allows the body to become a gateway to liberation and the source of true wholeness. It's the willingness to be intimate with the raw energetic experience of each wave as it appears—before it has been named as *headache, toothache, life-threatening pain,* or *incurable illness*—that transforms the darkness of "my suffering" into the illumination of being. By being deeply intimate with *all* manifestations, it's as if the boundaries of subject (you) and object (the manifestation) merge into a unified field of energy. This is more than metaphorical: there's a very real sense of disappearance into an inner dimension of light. It's not the light you see with your eyes, but a felt sense of lightness and peace.

It is this light that animates you. Without it your body would be an empty shell. You could also call this light the *Holy Spirit* (or simply *spirit*) or *God*. But because the word *God* often comes with religious and cultural baggage, you may prefer to simply call it *consciousness*. Whichever name you choose to call it, this light is the luminosity of an intelligence that exists prior to thinking or feeling. Even though its essential nature is not of this earthly dimension of form, it is the source of life in you and in everything. Beneath and beyond every manifestation is the limitless and deathless dimension of the unmanifest. While the unmanifest is often referred to as emptiness, it is far from empty (at least in the way the mind likes to think of it). It's an emptiness scintillating with unborn potential. Everything that is created, everything that is born into the world of appearances emanates from the omnipresent field of infinite possibilities. In this way, the inner world of light (the unmanifest) and the outer world of form (the manifest) are inseparable. Spirituality calls this *the Akashic field* or *Brahman*; science calls it *the zero-point field* or *implicate order*.

But don't take these words as gospel truth, or attempt to decipher them with logic, spiritual knowledge, or scientific evidence. Instead, discover for yourself what is truly inside every appearance when you rest deep inside it. Watch what happens when there's a cease-fire of ego's habit of censoring every sensation and feeling—when you stop naming pain, trauma, or illness, when you stop labeling as good or bad or spiritual or unspiritual, and when you stop framing as better or worse or as blessing or punishment. The invitation is for you to profoundly relax into the core of what is present *here and now* and to discover for yourself what remains when all appearances disappear into the lightness of being.

It is very likely that being fully present *in* the body (or, rather, in the deeper energy field of the body) brings not only the peace of an ineffable presence, but also a great lightness to the physical form. And it is very likely that you will experience greater vitality, vibrancy, and a sense of well-being and joy.

PURIFICATION OF THE BODY-TEMPLE

The idea that we can become more spiritual by adopting a certain physical practice is a popular one. Many people believe that following a specific diet (often based on moral or ethical grounds) or adopting a strict regimen of physical exercises (often based on an Eastern tradition) will elevate consciousness. It's true that certain activities—such as Sufi whirling, ecstatic dancing, repetitive deep breathing, long-distance running, advanced yogic postures, and long periods of fasting—can temporarily switch off the seeking mechanism of the egoic mind and allow a glimpse of your unbounded essential nature. And all of these activities can certainly provide support for a healthy and wholesome life. But, just as no one became enlightened by escaping the body, no one became enlightened by concentrating on the body.

In the deepest dimension of being and realm of inner light, the pristine purity of consciousness can neither be cleansed nor polluted by anything you do (or don't do) in the outer realm of physical form. Consciousness is like the sun; it can never be switched off. And yet, just as the sun's rays are refracted or weakened as they filter through dark clouds or hazy sky to cast shadows on the earth, the emanation of your inner light gets distorted or dissipated as it expresses itself through your earthly vehicle. While this distortion of the purity of your essential nature ultimately has no substance (just like a shadow has no real substance but is simply the absence of light), it does have a very real impact on you and your life.

The shadow is a representation of everything you hold in unforgiveness: the places where you refuse to let go of an archaic mechanism of defense and attack. These are the grievances (such as resentment, regret, blame, self-righteousness, or self-pity) that uphold the scaffolding of "me." When the raw energy inside each story of grievance remains unmet, these shadow-energies accumulate into a kind of emotional and physical debris. Unacknowledged rage, unexpressed grief, and unresolved trauma very often manifest as muscular tension, digestive disorders, metabolic imbalances, and unexplained aches and pains. If these shadow-energies continue to be ignored, they may eventually manifest as a more serious physical disharmony and disease. The body is a storehouse of the stories we hold in our minds, and every unexamined story is an additional encumbrance that obstructs the clarity of our unbounded nature as it is expressed through our earthly lives. If the light of consciousness is to flow unimpeded into our everyday reality, attention must be given to the unburdening of this repository of darkness.

In the ancient Aramaic text of the Gospel of Peace, Jesus speaks of a "cleansing of man's sins" in order to cast out the darkness of sorrow, fear, and disease. He refers to the body as "the temple of spirit" and counsels those that gather around him to purify the temple so that "Satan may not enter."[7] Do not be alarmed at the mention of Satan; this is not a sermon on Jesus's teachings, nor a treatise on spiritual purification! I invite you instead to read these words without the overlay of religious dogma. The cleansing of our sins really has nothing to do with being born morally impure, nor with any suggestion that you should follow a strict set of religious doctrines in order to "enter the kingdom of heaven." It has to do with the "missing of the mark" when you forget your true nature as wholeness and turn away from the luminous intelligence that breathes life into you. Another way of saying it is this: when you forget to be present in the body.

Without presence, it's as if you vacate the premises and leave the door wide open for uninvited guests. These unwelcome visitors are the polluted thoughts, toxic feelings, and unwholesome lifestyle behaviors that disturb your inner sanctum of peace and distract you from resting in the deeper stream of innate intelligence. This lack of presence also leaves your body susceptible to intrusive energies from the environment. On the psychic level these are low-vibration thought-forms, such as anger, fear, and judgment. On the physical level, these are micro-organisms, such as bacteria, viruses, and environmental pollutants found in water, food, and air, which lodge themselves in the delicate energy channels and in tissues, glands, bones, and blood. Jesus calls the accumulation of these shadow-energies *Satan*. Eastern traditions call this condition *stagnation, congestion, phlegm,* or *internal wind* (in Chinese medicine), and *tamas* or *ama* (in Ayurvedic medicine). Familiar Western terminology is *toxicity* and *inflammation*. We may also call it *low immunity* or *metabolic impairment*. Bloating, constipation, physical stiffness, mental fogginess, frequent colds, skin conditions, and a whole host of common ailments are early signs of this kind of invasion.

Purification of the body is like spring-cleaning your home. First you must be fully present, and then you must turn your attention to the removal of stagnant mental, emotional, and physical energies. The body is a gateway to a luminous whole-ness. Your willingness to sit inside all previously unmet ener-gies, as a felt sense *here and now*, is the beginning of a realignment with the flow of life's intelligence. Very often, simply being present with the deeper energetic experience of physical tension, discomfort, or pain dissolves the shadow by revealing the story inside it. If you are able to see that the story has no real substance in the light of conscious presence, you are likely to fall into the deeper dimension of the body, where the pristine light of your essential nature will offer you physical and psychic immunity.

When shadow-energies are particularly dense or stuck, you are required to dig deeper. There are many tools available from ancient and modern systems that enable us to excavate dark corners and to release, refresh, and rejuvenate the mind, heart, and body. Some intelligent strategies for supporting inner sanc-tity and sanity are:

cellular detoxification (using medicinal herbs and clays, sweating, and purgation), to remove physical toxins and reduce inflammation

regular physical movement, to keep the lymphatic system flowing and clear

skilled body-work (using deep-tissue massage and pressure points), to relax long-held tension and trauma emotional release techniques (such as deep breathing, whole-body shaking, primal screaming, and a myriad of other body-centered methods), to let go of old hurts, release buried feelings, and dissolve addictions

Even Jesus, in the Gospel of Peace, clearly outlined the "cleansing of man's sins" as a short but intense period of detoxification of body, heart, and mind through fasting, deep breathing, purgation, abstinence from addictive substances and behaviors, and solitary time for contemplation and prayer in nature. It's an ancient and timeless wisdom, born of the womb of the sacred feminine, which honors the inherent holiness and wholeness of earth and all earthly manifestations. It's not about perfecting your outer form, but about preparing an inner sanctuary where God (or Holy Spirit or the light of consciousness) can reside.

While purification of the body-temple does not cause or guarantee enlightenment, it *is* a useful preparation. Very often the light of awakeness is not strong enough to penetrate the denser forms of emotional and physical debris. Even if the aperture to awakeness opens, to afford a glimpse of the radiance of being (as in sudden awakening experiences), it can easily and quickly be hidden from view again. When awakening becomes a more permanent reality, as this light descends into heart and body, the encounter with shadow-energies can cause all sorts of problems if the process of embodiment is not fully engaged with. Extreme tiredness, unusual or unexpected physical pain and symptoms, involuntary spasms and shaking, sleeplessness, and intense body heat can all be experienced and are often not recognized as energetic blockages.

It's important to recognize that awakening kick-starts the spring-cleaning, and any attempt to avoid getting your hands dirty in the mire and muck of what has been unconscious in you, up until now, is like trying to pull down the blinds after the storm has blown through your house. A more intelligent response is to participate in the spring-cleaning by consciously engaging with it by being willing to discover what is asking to be released, by being willing to use the tools for purification, and by doing what it takes to support the growth of the bud of awakening into the flower of awakeness.

CELLULAR ENLIGHTENMENT

When we speak of an inner body of light, or of embodying the light, it is not merely a metaphorical statement, and neither is it just a metaphysical one. It's a description of a physical reality: we are literally made of light. Many ancient cultures (such as indigenous Aboriginal Australians and Native Americans) and many Eastern traditions of medicine and healing (such as Traditional Chinese Medicine and Ayurveda), as well as some esoteric traditions (such as the Kabbalah and Alchemy), have known that the body draws light from the macrocosm of the universe and distributes it through the energy meridians of the body to the microcosm of the organs, tissues, and cells. While this knowledge has been mostly forgotten, there is increasing evidence today (at least in some areas of medicine and science) that every cell of the human body has the capacity to store, utilize, and create light. And, more important, that the movement of light in and out of each cell is crucial to the health, vitality, and harmony of the body. This movement of light in the body has been called by various names: *chi, shakti, mana, universal life-force,* and *holy breath* are just some of the names used over the ages by different cultures.

Once again, as in previous pages, what follows here is not to be taken as irrefutable fact; there is plenty of historical, scientific, and spiritual literature that you can find if you are thirsty for knowledge about this topic. The invitation offered here is for you to simply relax into beingness, *here and now,* and hear these words from an inner silence. The more you relax, the more you inhabit your body. And it is in the fabric of your body that an inner knowingness is available. Here, in your innermost being, you do not need to seek evidence from an external authority. You simply know what is true because it resonates.

I invite you to take a pause for a moment, right here. Breathe deep into your belly and relax. Gently release your attention from any attempt to either grasp on to or reject the words on this page; in other words, turn your attention away from thinking. The invitation here is for you to enter an inner abode of light. You can sense this light, not with your physical eyes, but because it has a quality of silence, spaciousness, stillness, and a subtle, scintillating aliveness. And even though it is absolutely silent, it is this inner body of light that informs you, because light *is* life's intelligence.

As you rest here, be open to the possibility that light is carrying, in *this* moment, information from one cell to another, in order to keep the function of the endocrine system (the glands that regulate hormones) and all the organs (liver, kidneys, heart, nervous system, and so on) in alignment with diurnal rhythms; that is, the day-night cycle. It's a constant and precise ebb and flow of cleansing (the outflow) and nourishment (the inflow), just like the tides of the ocean, that allows us to rest and regenerate at night, and to wake up refreshed and reenergized in the morning. There's a whole body of research that reveals the complex biochemical interactions involved in this process, but it is not the purpose of this book to supply you with this information. The invitation is for you to allow these words to resonate in your inner knowingness, and pause here for a moment to open to the mystery of how this delicate dance does not require you to take charge of it, because it is perfectly orchestrated by the innate intelligence of light. Waking up tired, sluggish, or mentally foggy is a sign that the flow of light has been interrupted. Disease, especially if it is chronic, is a sign that the instrument through which this light flows has been damaged.

Now consider including in your inner investigation that recent discoveries in the field of advanced biology support the ancient wisdom of an inner body of light. This research shows that tiny light particles known as *biophotons* are released by DNA and then held in the cell membrane, in clusters known as *electron clouds.* The more electron clouds that gather, the more permeable the cell membrane is, and the more permeable the membrane, the more light passes through, with vital information from both the internal environment of the body-mind (the microcosm) and the external environment (the macrocosm) of the world and the universe. It is estimated that the human body is made of up 100 trillion cells, each one with a membrane that acts as a portal for information. This intricate system of cellular membranes is the communications highway of the body, allowing the light of universal intelligence to regulate the myriad of metabolic pathways necessary for a healthy life.

Further discoveries also show that the cell membrane is highly sensitive to the acid-alkaline balance of the fluid surrounding it. There is a delicate relationship between hydration, body temperature, and pH, and many chronic illnesses are known to correlate with an imbalance of these three factors. In order for electron clouds to be held at an optimal level in the cell membrane, the pH has to be just right. If the balance tips too far into acidity, the electron clouds dissipate, light diminishes, and the information relayed through the body is distorted. We could say that the cell has literally become "endarkened." We could also say (on a metaphysical level) that the shadow has set in. This kind of acidic internal environment is created by physical pollutants ingested in food and water or through the air, stress, fear, and unresolved emotions, and eventually this leads to disease.

Ancient systems of health (such as Traditional Chinese Medicine and Ayurveda) have long understood this and have developed specific techniques for deep cellular purification and deep cellular renourishment, to return the pH to its natural state at slightly alkaline. Recent discoveries show that a slightly alkaline environment increases cell permeability and attracts more electron clouds. On a physical level, more light is stored in the cell membrane. On a metaphysical level, we could say that each cell becomes en-lightened. Light can now move freely in and out of the cell, in tandem with circadian rhythms, and you literally become radiant with the luminosity of consciousness! This is a physiological reality in which *you*, as the expression of consciousness through a body-mind vehicle, dance in harmony with the totality. Once again, many ancient traditions have known about this phenomenon; some of the names given to it are the *rainbow body, golden aura,* and *kundalini awakening.* We could also simply call it *cellular enlightenment.*

Far from being a supernatural state, cellular enlightenment is your natural state. Another way of saying it is this: it's what exists prior to physical or psychic pollution, or that which exists before the shadow sets in. You could also say it's that which is in right relationship with its inner and outer environment, or that through which innate intelligence flows unimpeded. Most animals, especially those in the wild, exhibit this natural state of unity of body, beingness, and environment, as do many ancient indigenous cultures untouched by civilization (although not many of these exist today). Certainly in animals, this natural harmony is not fully conscious; it is simply the way life is. What is so different today, in the complex and often disharmonious modern world in which we live, is our capacity to fully engage with the process of cellular enlightenment. We engage with it by saying an unadulterated *yes* to the meeting of all shadow-energies, by the willingness to do what it takes to release all physical and psychic pollutants, and by being unwaveringly present in the body.

As you begin to fully participate in the process of cellular enlightenment, consciousness becomes conscious of itself through every cell. Each cell is a living entity unto itself; you are, in fact, not a single organism but a *community* of cells. Healthy communication between cells is vital if the community is to function as a harmonious whole. When each cell in a community is enlightened, whether it is *you* as an individual or a cell in your body, a new world is born. Could it be that this new world, whether it's an awakened humanity or the radiant glow of your light-body, is the foundation for an evolutionary leap in which the universe itself becomes conscious of itself?

THE ART OF CONSCIOUS EATING

The inquiry into the role of the body in living the truth of awakening in everyday life would not be complete without a conversation about food, or, more accurately, a conversation about our *relationship* to food.

This conversation has nothing to do with adhering to an ethically, morally, or even spiritually correct diet. Very often, being vegetarian (or vegan or fruitarian) is equated with being spiritual, but this is not necessarily so. While there are many good reasons for following this kind of diet, there can be a subtle judgment of others who choose a different way of eating. Often, this turns into righteousness, and the ego, rather than dissolving, is actually strengthened. This conversation also does not have anything to do with following specific advice about nutrition or health. There are no guidelines given here, no dos and don'ts, and no information or knowledge to titillate the mind. (There is plenty of this available on the Internet and in books if you wish to investigate the topics of nutrition and health.)

What is offered here is the invitation to go deeper than any belief or ideology, to stop making diet a religion, and to devote yourself to an authentic inquiry that brings attention to the *how* and *why* of eating. Discover for yourself what your body needs for the kind of nourishment that enlightens each cell and brings harmony to the cellular community. It's a journey that invites you to expose the mental and emotional maneuvers that cover over the innocent impulse of hunger.

The impulse to respond to hunger is, of course, hardwired into our physiology to ensure survival of the physical form, as it is in all living creatures. But in humans, unlike in most other living forms (some animals kept as pets are an exception), this natural mechanism has become hijacked by the ego's attempt to seek fulfillment from external forms.

Food nourishes us on many levels. It fuels the myriad metabolic processes of the body, and it also provides emotional satiation (a sense of grounding and fullness), feeds our soul by delighting our senses, and connects us to the bounty of the earth. There's nothing wrong with any of this. A multifaceted kind of nourishment is a part of our holistic nature. But when deriving psychological comfort from food is the primary driver of eating behavior, the relationship to food becomes unconscious. It is propelled by the addictive movement of the egoic mind, and like all addictions it obscures the deeper intelligence of our true nature and creates suffering. This suffering may manifest as an uncontrollable urge to binge or eat junk food, or an eating disorder such as bulimia or anorexia. Or it may end up as a digestive imbalance, as the discomfort of being overweight or sluggish, or as a diet-related disease.

Perhaps you do not suffer from any inconvenient or uncomfortable conditions, and have not given much thought to your relationship to food. Or maybe you are happy with your "healthy diet" and have no wish to investigate it further. But if you truly wish to fully embody the light of awakeness, you are invited to include your relationship to food in the spiritual inquiry. It's not just about preventing disease or maintaining good health; it's about building a light-vessel to carry consciousness on its earthly journey.

The honest investigation of *why* you eat the way you eat is the starting point for loosening the layers of conditioned responses that wrap themselves around the impulse of hunger. Are you willing to ask yourself these questions? Do you notice yourself reaching for the biscuit tin or box of chocolates when you're feeling low, hurt, or alone? Do you notice yourself piling the food onto your plate or gulping your food down when you're angry or upset? Do you place a high value on family meals, social gatherings centered around food, dinner celebrations, and romantic dinners as ways to feel connected, loved, and nurtured? Is it possible that the craving for sugary or starchy food is an attempt to suppress pain? Is it possible that eating too much and too fast is a way of stuffing down uncomfortable feelings? Is it possible that the high emphasis on social eating is a substitute for real fulfillment?

While enjoying food with family, friends, a lover, or simply alone is a wonderful part of the human experience, if unexamined it can become an avoidance of facing a deeper lack of nourishment. What's important here is not *what* you do but *why* you do it. Turning your attention to this inquiry allows you to see the addictive mechanism of seeking wholeness through something outside yourself. If you are willing to stop following this addictive mechanism, unconscious eating patterns are likely to lose their impetus. Once these patterns have been honestly seen and dissolved in the torchlight of awareness, all rules about *what* you eat become redundant. Instead of following a dietary protocol, you are guided by an innate intelligence that informs the present-moment choice of what and when to eat. This intelligence reveals itself when you slow down around the action of eating—before, during, and after.

Before you automatically reach for the leftovers in the fridge, grab take-out, or order the most tantalizing cake on the menu, slow down and breathe into your belly, be present with any sensations or emotions that reveal themselves, allow a more authentic hunger to arise, and simply *feel* this without moving away from it. As you prepare your meal, slow down and breathe into your belly, relax your senses, and be present with the shape and color and aroma of the food. Simply *be* with it, and resist the temptation to consume it. As you sit down with your plate, slow down and breathe, be present with the sensation of the food as each forkful enters your mouth. Slow down and be intimate with the taste and texture as you chew and swallow. When every morsel has been enjoyed, don't rush to get up, but simply wait, at least for a few moments, and breathe gently into your belly, allowing the feeling of fulfillment to be absorbed into every cell, into mind and heart and belly. This is the art of conscious eating.

The art of conscious eating has nothing to do with "doing the right thing," but everything to do with falling in love with each moment of the act of eating. It's not indulgent; it's sacred. It's an incredibly intimate act, a communion in which you take into yourself another form. And, in the fire of digestion, it is transmuted into nourishment for the benefit of the form called *you*. When eating is no longer driven by an emotional hunger but by a hunger for the radiance of wholeness, nourishment comes from a deeper source than the material form. It comes from light itself.

Some forms are more light-filled than others, and when you are purified of mental and emotional motives for eating, you become exquisitely sensitive to this. This sensitivity is not knowledge-based, but a kind of cellular sensing in which you feel the vibrational difference between mass-produced, factory-farmed, artificially grown, highly processed foods and fresh, naturally grown whole foods. You feel it through your eyes, nostrils, taste buds, stomach, and through your invisible energy-body (or *aura*). This felt sense, when fully opened to, also brings an exquisite sensitivity to the raw reality of consuming another life form (whether it is animal or vegetable or fruit) in order to sustain our own lives. In the bittersweet acceptance of the inextricable relationship between life and death, we are offered a moment of honoring the sacredness of all life.

Many people ask if eating meat or animal products has its place on the spiritual path. This is a valid question if we are to become more conscious, and especially in today's world of mass farming. Although there are countless arguments for and against it, there is no ultimate answer to this. The deeper invitation of this question is for you to discover for yourself what is true for *you* by eating consciously. Whether you are a vegetarian, vegan, or an avid meat-eater, be willing to have all judgments of yourself and of others exposed. Be willing to see where you take a moral, ethical, nutritional, or spiritual stand for one way of eating over another. And then be willing to open to a new possibility that has no stance in it. Be present, slow down, and breathe as you fill up your shopping basket at the supermarket, as you rush to the fridge, as you pile up your plate, and as you take in the next mouthful. Perhaps you will discover that what harms you (as well as what harms other life-forms and the environment) is not what you eat but *how* you eat it. It's an unconscious relationship to food that is the cause of disease and disharmony in your body and in the planetary body. If you rest in the tenderness of your heart and in the intelligence of your gut, you will *feel* what is true for you. You will be guided to make new choices that no longer endarken the cells of your body or reinforce the suffering created on earth by inhumane animal farming, chemical overload, and desecration of land.

In the intimacy of each bite and chew, perhaps you will be touched by the recognition that eating is a sacred act of beauty.

You may be moved to give thanks from the depths of your innermost being and offer a blessing for the life that is given in order to give *you* life. Whether the life given is animal, vegetable, or fruit, your conscious blessing of it not only nourishes you on a deeper level, but it also releases the karmic bondage of life and death. This way, you and the life-form that has sacrificed itself for you are transformed by the wholeness and holiness of love.

DISSOLVING ADDICTIONS

We often think of addiction as a physical or mental illness, but it's actually a condition of the unilluminated mind. Whether it's the need to get high on drugs or alcohol, the habit of cigarette smoking, the temptation of comfort-eating, the allure of sexual encounters, the excitement of gambling, or the compulsion for surfing the Internet, it is ego's endless craving for something *more* to avert the discomfort of incompleteness. The continuous movement—from perceived lack to perceived fulfillment, from disillusionment, to longing for fulfillment, to looking for something that will satisfy this longing—underpins the repetitive behavior we call addiction.

You may not see yourself as an addict, but as long as this mechanism remains unexamined in you, it is the driver for most of your actions, even the most harmless ones. Ego's unconscious impulse to seek fulfillment in the external realm of form is what drives the vast proportion of human activity, including the jobs and careers we pursue, the relationships we desire, the accumulation of material wealth, the pattern of our social interactions, and the need for entertainment. It also includes our everyday decisions, such as what and when to eat, what to buy, what to do during our "spare time," whether to have another bottle of beer or one more piece of cake, make another phone call to a friend, or read yet another spiritual book … and so on.

Perhaps you are wondering, if it's harmless, why should I be concerned with whether it's called an addiction? Of course, there is nothing essentially wrong with eating cake, drinking beer, connecting with friends, watching a movie, or making money. All of these activities are innocent in themselves and a normal part of the engagement with everyday life. The problem is not *what* you seek, but the reason that you seek it. It's the seeking mechanism itself that is the problem, because it hijacks your decisions and gives the illusion of conscious choice when, in fact, you are unconsciously acting out ego's commands. Since the ego is restless (always running away from or toward something), you are caught in an endless cycle of suffering, and this *is* harmful.

Let's take a moment to investigate this. You're going about your day as usual. You're calm and everything happens smoothly. You may be feeling good or happy, and you may even be smiling. There's a sense of satisfaction or completeness, because you're not wanting anything to be different from how it is. And then, seemingly out of nowhere, you notice a growing discomfort. Perhaps there's a negative internal dialogue in the back of your mind or a tension in the pit of your stomach. Maybe this change in you is triggered by something that happens: a difficult phone call, an unexpected bill in the mail, you drop coffee all over your favorite shirt, or you stub your toe getting out of the bath. Or there appears to be no cause; it's just a certain mood or feeling that comes over you. (Undoubtedly, there is a thought or memory that has triggered this feeling, but you may not be aware of it.) Now you don't feel so good, you're no longer happy, and there's a sense of dissatisfaction and incompleteness. Then, again, seemingly out of nowhere, an urge arises in you: you want a chocolate biscuit, a frothy double latte, a cigarette, a glass of whiskey, or perhaps you feel compelled to surf the Internet or go out shopping. You follow this urge and surrender to it, and there is relief. The discomfort disappears, the wanting dissipates, and for a few moments or longer you feel satiated or complete. You no longer want anything to be different than how it is. The relief happens because you surrender. The separate "me" temporarily dies, and you become one with the object of your desire. The problem is that this is not a real death; real death happens when egoic identification dissolves into the formless dimension of being. But by surrendering to the impermanent nature of form, the separate "me" inevitably reappears, and so you feel incomplete again and a new desire arises.

The suffering of the addictive cycle is magnified if there is a particularly intense sense of incompleteness, such as a pattern of repetitive personal wounding from childhood trauma, a betrayal or lack of safety, some kind of denial or deprivation, a major disappointment or devastating loss, or harsh living conditions. When the discomfort of facing the sense of incompleteness becomes too much to bear, the object of desire tends to be more all-consuming. When the repetitive nature of satisfying this desire becomes more compulsive (such as smoking or gambling), or when the object of desire is harmful to the physiological vehicle (such as excessive alcohol or cocaine), there is likely to be a detrimental impact on physical health, relationships, social interactions, and work. We call this an addiction and classify it as an illness.

What usually follows is an attempt to find ways to stop the addiction: detoxification, medication, psychotherapy, behavioral reprogramming, and group therapy. While some or all of these methods may be a useful support, most often they do not work as a long-term solution, because none of these interventions get to the root of the problem. What is overlooked here is that addiction is not an illness of the body or of the brain, but a disease of the soul. It's a sign of the forgetting of your true nature as wholeness, and the misguided attempt to return to it by looking for wholeness in something outside of yourself.

Whether it's the seemingly harmless desire for chocolate or the more obviously harmful desire for a heroin fix, the problem—and the solution—is essentially the same. The problem is the addictive mechanism of the horizontal mind. The solution is the clear-seeing of this mechanism. Clear-seeing has nothing to do with a visual clarity, nor with the understanding of the intellect. It's what happens when you are fully present in the urge, when you stop running away from agonizing discomfort and instead choose to stay present with it, and when you feel the horror of your sense of lack and sit inside it without trying to change it. It's an open and tender space that allows the underlying pain of incompleteness to reveal itself. Of course, it is often too difficult to be fully present to, and support may be needed to unravel some of the complexities around the more harmful addictions and to help develop the capacity to bring awareness to what is driving the addictive behavior.

After all the support has been taken and all the unraveling has been done, it is only *presence* that can dissolve addiction. Whatever the circumstances of your life, your history, whatever loss, abuse, or neglect was the catalyst for your addiction, and whatever the actual substance, activity, or person you're addicted to, it is only your 100 percent willingness to stop giving your allegiance to the seeking mechanism that can truly change anything. In this willingness to stop, right here in *this* moment, even if there is an overwhelming wanting of something, there is the possibility to discover what is always complete, whether your craving is satisfied or not. This discovery is an intimacy with *now,* and this is what your craving has really been pointing to all along. It's the longing to come home to the fullness of this present moment, because you are, in fact, inseparable from this moment. What you have been looking for, over and over again, is right *here* in your innermost being as the depth of *you.*

You may be wondering, does all wanting dissolve in the fullness of this moment, when you discover the truth of your innate wholeness? Do you become detached from all human desires? Are you still able to choose whether to have a cup of tea or a cup of coffee, to go on the dinner date or just stay at home, to write that book gestating in your belly or just get a job at the local supermarket? How in the world are you meant to make a decision if there is no more wanting of anything to be other than how it is now?

The idea that in fully realizing our true nature we stop having any choice-making ability is a prevalent one in some spiritual circles, but it's an idea that arises out of an unilluminated mind. What actually happens, if there is an authentic awakening to your true nature, is a falling away of all desires that arise out of a sense of lack. Sometimes this is sudden, but most often it is gradual. It's the end of any attempt to gain or possess something more in order to feel complete. What remains is an innocent wanting, arising either as the body's natural impulse to respond to hunger, as a playful desire for chatting with a friend, as a gentle turning inward to solitude, or as a preference for tea over coffee, and so on. What changes is not that you stop having the capacity to make choices, nor that you stop enjoying the delights of the earthly dimension, but that there is freedom in getting what you want and freedom in not getting what you want.

MEETING PAIN, ILLNESS, AND DEATH

It is not a surprise that one of the greatest obstacles to being fully present is the experience of pain, especially if it is severe. Whether you're a longtime spiritual seeker or a newcomer to spiritual inquiry, pain is a challenge to the notion of "I am not the body." It is often a shock and a disappointment to the newly awakened mind when pain, either because of accident or illness, reminds us of the immediacy and fragility of our earthly existence. If there is any attempt to deny the reality of this direct experience, a cascade of spiritual statements is likely to come rushing in, to fortress against the shattering of cherished ideas of how awakening looks and feels.

At one of my gatherings, someone asked why I had a big bandage on my finger. I replied that I had gone to the hospital early that morning to have emergency stitches. He then asked, with genuine surprise in his voice, why, as a spiritual teacher, I had responded to pain or even been remotely concerned with the body. I replied that the finger had been bleeding profusely throughout the night. In being fully present with the reality of the situation, I simply did what needed to be done; there was no story in this.

Statements such as "Pain is an illusion," "There's nobody here," "There's nothing happening," and "Suffering does not exist" are very attractive to the seeker of nondual truth. But if these ideas remain unexamined in the present-moment reality of pain, this so-called truth is a barrier to true freedom. In every moment, pain (whether through injury or illness) offers us the opportunity to discover what is truly untouched and unharmed. It's a potent invitation to conscious surrender.

If you are willing to discover what is more true than any concept of nonduality and more real than any image of awakening, the horror of admitting that there is suffering must first be faced. To admit to suffering is to admit to being human, and this is often anathema to the spiritual seeker who harbors an expectation of a pain-free life. The belief that there should be no pain, when there blatantly *is* pain, is a very common spiritual bypassing tactic. In the attempt to be free, you create a subtle bondage: the erroneous belief that awakening transcends pain. What liberates you is the naked reality of it. Should there be pain? Yes. Why? Because it *is*—simply and utterly—here.

The admitting of suffering is an entry-point to the heart. It's an opportunity to expose all the uncomfortable and unspiritual feelings that must be faced if true freedom and healing are to be discovered. Most often, especially if pain is severe, this means facing fear, rage, grief, helplessness, and aloneness. These stormy clouds invite you to fully *feel* where feeling has been previously denied. If you are willing to fully feel, without any reservation (in other words, with an intensity of presence), the heart breaks open wider than the pain and the suffering, into an unadulterated acceptance of what is. Although the reality of your circumstances must be accepted before any real transformation can take place, the admitting of suffering has nothing to do with resigning yourself to the circumstances of your life, but everything to do with an inner state of nonresistance. If nonresistance is total, it brings an end to suffering.

Perhaps you can now see how suffering is a means to an end, not the end itself. It is simply the doorway to surrender. Suffering invites you to sacrifice the addictive movement of mind in the present moment, however agonizing or terrifying. You may be genuinely willing to surrender to the relatively short-lived pain of toothache or headache or wounded finger. But maybe the horror of a life-threatening illness is more challenging, and this is where you are asked to sacrifice much more than you are comfortable with. This sacrifice is necessary if there is to be any freedom within this unwelcome circumstance.

Very often, when illness arrives, either suddenly or gradually, there is an unquestioned attempt to suppress symptoms, whether it be with painkillers, medication, or even surgery. The desire to get rid of what is diseased and to fix what is damaged is a very natural response to keeping the body alive. Certainly, from the perspective of ego, illness is a disaster. It's a threat not only to the physical life-form but also to the whole construct of "my life." As long as the attempt to hold on to life remains unexamined, there cannot be true healing.

Medical intervention is very often a necessary part of the healing process. It's really not about rejecting support where needed. Painkillers, medication, and surgery can all be included in this, because even though these options seem like unnatural interventions, there is a divine intelligence at the source of all manifestations. The conversation offered here is not about what you choose to do, but about the invitation to stop and listen to the deeper intelligence that sits inside all physical symptoms before following the reactivity of the survival mechanism. It's an invitation to meet the emotional and mental contractions that are an integral part of the manifestation of physical disease, and that are easily avoided when attention is given only to surface manifestations. It's here, in the deepest dimension of being, that true healing lies. I invite you to consider that healing is not necessarily the absence of illness or pain, but the absence of the story of "poor me" within the illness or pain.

If you are suffering from any kind of illness, pain, or debility, I invite you to take a pause for a moment, right here. Breathe deep into your belly and relax. Gently release your attention from any attempt to fix your symptoms, to understand the cause of your condition, or to choose the right thing to do. Simply be here, fully present with what is. Are you willing, at least in *this* moment, to discover what is at the heart of all manifestations, however horrible or terrifying? Are you truly willing to discover what is more enduring than the experience of pain or illness, and what is more enduring than your physical form?

Illness is an invitation to meet every wave of painful sensation, excruciating emotion, and tormenting thought in tender openness and in innocent curiosity. Inevitably, stories of past and future will come tumbling in: "What did I do wrong?" "How long will this last?" "Is my life over?" "Will I be sick and in pain forever?" "Will I be an invalid?" And so on. These are not to be avoided. Instead, the invitation is to allow all stories of failure and calamity into the light of awareness, to open to the dazzling horror of it all without investing a "poor me" in it.

It is also inevitable that every image of yourself, such as mother or father, husband or wife, entrepreneur or artist, will be ruthlessly challenged. How can any of these roles survive in the face of "the end of my life," and who are you without these roles? If you believe yourself to be a spiritual person, or if you think you are awakened or enlightened, you are likely to encounter intense disappointment as every construct that upholds this image is confronted in the face of "unspiritual" or "unenlightened" thoughts and feelings. The devastation of your role as a spiritual, awakened, or enlightened person is also not to be avoided. Instead, the invitation is to allow every image of yourself, even the idea that there is no "self," to be annihilated so that you can discover the truth of yourself. Not as "I am *this*" or "I am *that*," but simply as "I am."

Illness invites you to stop right here, in the nakedness of that which simply *is*. It's an end to the horizontality of time, in which past fear and future hope create a deep-seated restlessness and distress, and a fall into an eternal presence that invites you to discover what is already whole and at peace. At this deeper dimension of consciousness, whether the body survives or not is not of primary importance. What really matters is the possibility of resting within the truth of who you really are, beneath and beyond a "me" that is ill, damaged, cursed, unloved, or unspiritual.

Most likely, when this truth is recognized and welcomed into all unilluminated parts of mind, heart, and belly, there is a physical healing. This reversal of the disease process may happen suddenly, seemingly by divine intervention or grace, or it may happen gradually, perhaps with the support of conventional medical treatment or perhaps with natural and holistic therapies. Whichever way it happens, it's an indication of a realignment with innate intelligence, allowing light to infuse the 100 trillion cells of your body. However, sometimes the discovery of your true nature as consciousness can only be made in the final surrender to the body's dissolution. Although this may be in opposition to any idea of "a positive outcome," it is absolutely perfect, because in conscious surrender to death, it is the soul that is healed and not the physical shell. Whether the body survives or not, the intelligence that manifests as illness is a benevolent force, inviting you to open to the ever-present love at the core of all manifestations, even the most horrendous ones.

True healing is what happens when consciousness recognizes its own wholeness amid what appears to be broken or wounded. Are you willing to discover what is truly here, in both life and death? Are you willing to discover that there is only one beingness, which appears to be born into the fullness of a myriad of forms, and to die back into an immeasurable emptiness over and over again, in *this* moment and in *every* moment? Are you willing to die into the lightness of being ... *now?*

LIVING LIGHTLY ON THE EARTH

The willingness to die in every moment allows you to live lightly on the earth. Living lightly has an immense impact on personal and global peace. Today, amid increasingly disturbing and turbulent times, many people are asking if there is anything we should do to save the world. There are, of course, many valiant and worthwhile endeavors by individuals and groups to address the corruption and violence we see today. Some of these have been extremely successful in bringing awareness to the complex issues we face in the modern world, and have even provided effective solutions (at least on a local scale).

But none of this can be a long-term solution, because the responsibility for peace on earth lies deep within *you*. You are not required to fight the enemy, nor to campaign for social, political, or ecological justice. And you don't need to become a rebel, an activist, a leader, or an innovator, although any or all of these roles may be expressed through you at various times. Your responsibility is to know the truth of who you are, *as* consciousness, and to live this truth in every cell of your being, metaphorically and literally.

When all inner and outer manifestations, including *you*, are recognized as consciousness shining through form, all resistance to life in its glorious and horrific guises dissolves. Then the burden of carrying metaphorical weapons of destruction is put down. When you see yourself in everyone, there is no one to defend and no one to attack. Blame, judgment, righteousness, and all other divisive maneuvers are no longer required. Your awakening out of the dream of separation is the end of warfare. It's the end of overreactivity in the neurophysiology of the body, the end of power games in intimate relationship, and the end of the battle for supremacy between nations, creeds, and cultures.

Living lightly on the earth, and living *as* the light of consciousness, is the natural flow of compassion from an awakened heart to the heart of reality. It's not about saving the world, but about giving your devotion to the mystery of this moment as it expresses itself through everything. It's about living the truth of oneness within the preciousness of life and within the inevitability of death. All forms, including your body and the body of the planet, are destined to die. This death may be a gentle passing away, or it may be a violent storm. We cannot possibly know, and we certainly cannot control it. But we can rest deeply in the truth of peace, come what may.

Are you willing to stop the war right *here and now*? Are you willing to take responsibility for peace by being fully present in the luminosity of being, in *this* moment? If your answer is a deep *yes*, from your heart, your belly, and the aliveness of your cells, then you will have fulfilled your true purpose. And peace on earth, at least in *this* moment, is possible.

CHAPTER 10

Work, Money, and Living Your True Purpose

WHAT HAPPENS AFTER AWAKENING?

A common misconception in spiritual circles is that after awakening there is "nobody here" and therefore "nothing to do." This belief, when taken literally by the acquisitive mind, gives rise to a whole host of dilemmas. Some of the most common predicaments are: "If there's nobody here, who will make decisions?" "Will I lose interest in normal life and lose my job/marriage/friends/home/health?" "Will my life change for the worse, or for the better?" Other troublesome questions are: "Will the true purpose of my life just happen without me having to do anything?" and "Will synchronicity bring me everything I dream of in order to live a spiritual life?"

Many spiritual seekers, even those who report profound awakening experiences, are confused about what happens (or doesn't happen) after awakening. They speak a lot about "going with the flow" and "life is just happening," but very often these statements of absolute truth are not fully realized, and the depth of this truth cannot flow into everyday life. What these seekers are really referring to is surrender. Although surrender is often spoken of by spiritual teachers (including myself) as the key to spiritual freedom, somehow it has become erroneously equated with being passive. In other words, surrender is conveniently confused with "not doing anything." It's convenient because it upholds the idea that you can abdicate responsibility for making decisions or having a direction in life. This kind of surrender is really a laziness masquerading as spirituality. It's a subtle egoic strategy for staying in the comfort zone. It's not malicious or even intentional; it's simply a blind spot. It's what happens when the "I" that continues to operate after awakening is rejected, and is an indication that awakeness has not yet descended from mind to heart to belly.

When surrender gets stuck as a mental abstraction, there's a kind of constipation that prevents the maturation of awakening. What causes the blockage is a hidden agenda: the expectation that life after awakening is easy, there are no more challenges to grow from, you never stumble and fall and have to pick yourself up again, and you never have to harness an inner strength or discipline or resilience in order to fulfill your highest potential as a human being. There's also an expectation that only good things happen, no personal calamity ever strikes, and you're protected against the world's tragedy. This kind of superstitious thinking means you don't have to engage with the messy business of being human—that somehow, just because you're in the spiritually elevated zone of "going with the flow," nothing touches you. And anyway, even if things don't work out as smoothly as expected (say your partner suddenly leaves you or someone close to you dies), there's no "self" to be hurt or disappointed and there's no "self" to pick up the pieces or to make decisions. While this extreme nondual standpoint may seem to provide immunity from suffering, there's a lack of engagement with life that creates a more underground (and yet just as malignant) suffering called apathy.

True freedom from suffering happens when the "I" that is the doer is embraced as an integral expression of consciousness. At this deeper level of surrender, there is no longer an opposition between being and doing, because the outer action of doing (and making decisions) arises out of an inner silence of being. You can be very active and yet totally silent within. You could call this *awakened doing*. Or you can be very passive (or active) and yet incredibly noisy within. This is the *modus operandi* of the unawakened state and it is how humanity has been functioning for millennia (except for a few rare individuals throughout the ages).

In the mode of unawakened doing (or egoic doing), there's a belief that personal will (or the sense of "I") is a force that exists independently of life. This belief is either extremely empowering, because you think you are the creator of your reality, or extremely disempowering, because you think you are a victim of your reality. Usually, you oscillate between the two ends of the continuum, depending on whether life conforms to your wishes or not. Either way, there is no freedom or peace in this. This is the "living in the dream" state, but there is no real life in this because you are operating as an automaton, unconsciously reacting to ego's cravings and aversions.

In awakened doing, while the sense of an "I" that makes decisions continues, there's a very different quality. There's a sense of effortless effort, a kind of spontaneity that arises from being deeply rooted in the belly. You make decisions and take action (or nonaction) from a gut feeling. It's a direct moment-to-moment response to the waves that appear as part of the human experience. It's so instantaneous that there's no sense of personal will, and it *feels* as if you are "going with the flow." What's really happening is that there is no inner resistance to the deeper impulse of life's intelligence. It's as if each moment-to-moment unfoldment is happening at the same time as your response to it. Whether your response is a *yes* or a *no* is not the issue, because life's intelligence has already revealed the *yes* or the *no* through the "I" that appears to make a decision. You can tell if your doing arises out of being, because there is peace in the *yes* and peace in the *no*. In other words, there is no judgment or refusal of any decision or action that wants to move in you. But if your doing comes from ego, there is conflict with both the *yes* and the *no,* and you will doubt your gut instinct. This inner conflict is what creates suffering in you, and in those around you.

If you are willing to consciously surrender all nondual notions of "There is no one here to do anything," it's very likely that all troublesome questions about what happens (or doesn't happen) after awakening vanish into a deep acceptance of both that which is fully awake in you (the absolute) and that which is fully human (the relative). If you are willing to simply be at peace with what arises in you as *this* decision or *that* decision (or *this* action or *that* action), the unfoldment of your true life's purpose is just a hair's breadth away.

AWAKENING TO YOUR LIFE'S PURPOSE

Today, many people are looking for a deeper meaning and purpose to their life, especially if they are on some kind of self-development or spiritual path. As traditional roles of bread-winner and homemaker become less relevant (at least in the Western world), there's a growing dissatisfaction with the daily routine of making a living or pursuing a career without soul. It's highly likely, since you're reading this book, that you, too, are yearning to find a deeper purpose to your life, one that brings your true voice into the world and serves something more than day-to-day survival or material comfort.

Do you have a sweet sense of what makes your heart sing, but are unsure if this is your true purpose in life? Have you already discovered your unique talents, but are afraid to let go of the security of a regular job? Do you have a strong vision of what you'd like to do and how you'd like your life to be, but don't know where to begin? Or perhaps you've had a clear glimpse of awakening and are now wondering whether you should share this message with others, or whether you should write a book or become a spiritual teacher? While questions such as these are a part of the search for your authentic expression in the world, if you are to truly live your purpose you must first abandon all imaginations, hopes, and desires of what this purpose looks like. This may sound depressing, deflating, or counterproductive, but if you are willing to surrender (just for *this* moment) your vision of a brighter future for yourself, there is the possibility of a much deeper (and more lasting) fulfillment than anything you can imagine.

There's a tendency even in spiritual circles to believe that living your purpose is about manifesting your dream. This dream usually includes the desire to be creative, successful, happy, and abundant. And very often, this also includes the desire to make a unique contribution to the world or to help other people. There's really nothing wrong with any of this; it's all a part of living your true purpose in an earthly dimension. Usually, one (or more) self-help methods are employed to assist in the creation of your dream. There are many tools for clearing inner blocks to abundance, empowering yourself to stretch beyond your limitations, and manifesting the life you want. But however magnificent, magical, beautiful, or humanitarian your dream is, if there is any investment of self in this vision, it is bound to fail, sooner or later. When the power of creation is coopted by an unilluminated mind (a mind that does not know its own true nature as emptiness but believes itself to be the creator of reality), it re-creates the same delusion of self-importance and grasping that has created greed, corruption, and devastation in the world. It may be a more positive creation, but it is still built on an erroneous belief in the permanency of form. All forms are transient, even the most spiritual ones, and without an anchor in the deepest dimension of beingness that does not come and go, the vicissitudes of the world will threaten to wipe out the satisfaction, joy, and fulfillment derived from external manifestations.

Your true purpose and fulfillment have nothing to do with what you do or with what you imagine yourself to be, but everything to do with who you are beneath and beyond all forms. The invitation is to stop asking, "How can I manifest my dream of a better life?" or "How can I do something special/important/unique/spiritual in the world?" and to turn your attention to the primary purpose of your life: awakening out of the dream of separation. Your true purpose is an inner, not an outer, one. Without staying true to this, you will keep on chasing dreams.

If you are on a path of spiritual inquiry, your commitment to realizing your inner purpose prior to finding your outer purpose is likely, over time, to unravel all agendas and expectations of what you *should* be doing, what you *will* be doing, and even of what you *want* to be doing. This unraveling allows the revelation and release of an essential quality of beingness that wants to express itself through you *as* you. Not as a future dream, but as a present-moment reality. This quality of beingness exists prior to conditioning, and is experienced as a subtle felt-sense (such as clarity, playfulness, devotion, or harmony) when you are still and silent inside.

If you stay tenderly true to this quality of beingness by being absolutely present within it, without an agenda of becoming anything or any expectation of manifesting anything, something will prompt you from within. Initially, you may be unsure if this inner impulse is real, but if you are supremely still and silent, you will recognize it as the movement of innate intelligence. It doesn't run ahead with visioning, goals, or end results. It is rooted in the fullness of now and is guided by a gentle yet irrevocable *yes* in the belly. As it gives birth to your outer purpose (and this may come as a blinding insight, as a complete download of your mission, or as a slow revelation piece by piece), there's an alignment with life's evolutionary movement and a letting go of struggle or pushing to make things happen. It doesn't mean you become passive and just "go with the flow." It means there's no longer a need for self-empowerment rituals, positive affirmations, creative visualization, or the law of attraction. There's no need for you to manifest anything, because you, as a separate self, are no longer the creator of reality. The mystery that creates life (you can also call this *consciousness* or *God*) is.

Your outer purpose is also not static. In other words, it's not a fixed picture of the outcome or an image of yourself in your role as *this* or *that*. It's not a step-by-step journey from A to Z. It's a fluid unfoldment that has peaks and troughs, and no destination. If there is a deep acceptance of all of it, in whichever way it moves, there is a profound fulfillment here. You can be incredibly busy or incredibly still; either way, you are fulfilling your purpose.

Your purpose may, or may not, look the way you imagine or want it to be. If you have awakened, your life may, or may not, conform to any picture of an awakened or spiritual life. It's likely (although there is no guarantee) that the groove of your life will continue along the same lines as it always has. If you are naturally drawn to guiding others, it's possible that you will naturally take up the role of spiritual guide or mentor. If you are gifted with words, you may become a speaker or author. If you are artistic, it's probable that awakeness expresses itself through some form of art, poetry, or dance. If you are a natural entrepreneur, it's very likely you will devote yourself to a project or business that serves to uplift and awaken others. If you are happy working in a supermarket or gas station or tending the roses in the public garden, then the simplicity of your presence (and possibly your smile) will be the portal through which the light comes through. These are just some of the possibilities. There are many more. But it's not necessarily about the outer form, since this is likely to evolve over time. It's about an inner quality of being.

Awakeness does not care who you are as an individual with a story. Its nature is the same in all things and no one person is more special than another. Yet awakeness uses your personality vehicle to birth itself into the world. This is why each flower of awakeness is unique in its outer expression. For me, awakeness expresses itself through the weft and warp that have made up the complex and often dramatic tapestry of my life. The personality vehicle I have incarnated into has mostly been fragile and frequently brought to its knees by life's turmoil. But I see now that throughout it all there was (and continues to be) a disciplined mind and rebellious spirit. I have never been able to conform to society's rules about family, work, or career (often to my own detriment). Throughout my life, I have chosen to sacrifice comfort and security for freedom. Given the circumstances of my life and the choices that were inevitably made in response to these circumstances, it is not such a surprise that awakeness expresses itself through my role today as spiritual teacher and author.

I say all this, not to dwell on my story, but to give you a flavor of how awakeness moves through a human being. I do not know the twists and turns that make up the story of your life, or the nuances of personality that shape you into a unique human being. Nor do I know how awakeness will express itself through you or how your outer purpose will look. But I do know that when personal will (the "me" with all its wants and expectations) is finally laid down at the altar of divine will (the mystery of the unknown; you could also call this *the Holy Spirit* or *God*), an unstoppable force of vital aliveness moves through your life and gives you the courage to live without a safety net. You could also call this *the freedom of living selflessly.*

THE COURAGE TO LIVE SELFLESSLY

Many people (especially if they are on a spiritual path) want to live a life of service, to contribute something worthwhile to the world, and to live without the burden of self-centered accumulation of material wealth or profit at all cost. This isn't a surprise, as there's a freedom and fulfillment in living selflessly that speaks to the innocence of our hearts.

Most often, living selflessly is equated with doing good deeds or donating money to charity or being a philanthropist. This is a misdirection of attention, because it really has nothing to do with what you do; it's about surrendering the need to get anything back from what you do. This doesn't mean playing the martyr or the saint by denying yourself basic material comfort, safety, or pleasure. It doesn't mean you have to give away all of your skills, services, time, and energy for free. What is referred to here is the need to have an image of yourself reflected back by the world, or receive approval, recognition, love, or anything else that makes you feel special or worthy. Of course, there's nothing wrong with any of these feelings, they are beautiful waves in the ocean of consciousness and an inevitable part of living your outer purpose. But when there is an investment of self in these feelings, you become tied to the ebb and flow of the world, and this puts a brake on the flow of true abundance.

Giving in order to receive is often a very hidden defense mechanism. By making sure you get back a reflection of your own goodness, specialness, or worthiness, you are protected from being hurt by rejection, disapproval, or ridicule. It's a safety net, in case you stumble and fall. True selflessness is an unconditional self-exposure. It's the willingness to bare yourself to the world. It's about not withholding yourself from life, even if you feel ugly, weak, stupid, insecure, or worthless. It's about not knowing if you will be liked or disliked, if you will be adored or crucified, if you will succeed or fail. It's about falling in love with the unknownness of each unfolding moment, and giving yourself as openness.

There's an idea that just because you have awakened (and particularly if this awakening has stabilized as an abiding state), there's no more personal growth. While this is true at the absolute level of consciousness—because who you really are as consciousness is unchanging—on a relative earthly level, there's an inevitable evolution of the mind-body vehicle. This has less to do with being clever, confident, competent, or learning new skills (although it may include some or all of this), and more about a purification of remaining defensive structures that prevent your true light from shining forth. As you devote yourself to what is true in you and to the impulse for this to be expressed in the world as your outer purpose, life's intelligence nudges you beyond your comfort zone, putting you in situations that call for honesty, humility, and a gentle but unwavering inner authority. It's as if the sword of the Holy Spirit comes down to carve away what is superfluous in you, to refine any sharp edges, and to polish your earthly vehicle until it is transparent. When you can stand as openness in the face of the world's judgment and still give yourself totally, you will have discovered the true meaning of living selflessly.

In selflessness, even though your personality may continue to experience discomfort and challenge, the texture is very different from the kind of struggle that is experienced when your mind is set on an outcome. Feeling impatient, frustrated, or anxious is an indicator that you have slipped back into a self-centered or egoic mode of function. While this may occasionally happen, at least in the early stages, eventually you will learn to surf on the edge of surrender until every ounce of you finally stops trying to manifest what you want. You will come to know, in every fiber of your being, that you cannot manifest the mystery; the mystery manifests you.

TRANSFORMING WORK FROM BURDEN TO JOY

It's a common belief that work (what we do in order to make a living) and spirituality are incompatible. Work binds us to the material world, whereas spirituality frees us. This view is supported by traditional cultures, especially Eastern ones, in which turning attention to the spiritual path came only after a certain age when one's life's work is complete ("retirement") or as a complete renunciation of worldly life (monasticism). Women, in particular, if they were tied to the traditional role of child-bearer and homemaker, were even less likely to commit to a spiritual path. But today, as an increasing number of people of all ages, cultures, and backgrounds turn to spiritual inquiry, there's an evolutionary pull to find freedom within the marketplace of life. Of course, this throws up all sorts of inherited beliefs and inner conflicts.

Many people I meet at my gatherings believe that the work they do in order to make a living is in direct opposition to their spiritual path. Many feel trapped by their job or career and feel they don't have enough time or energy to be spiritual. Others avoid getting a job or following a career path because they're too busy being spiritual. Most often there's an underlying fear that awakening out of the dream of "me" means that ordinary life will become meaningless and they'll be unable to function in the office, boardroom, factory, or the kitchen.

There is a strong possibility that if you glimpse who you are beneath the roles you play in the everyday world, the work you do is clearly out of tune with your innermost truth. But don't take this possibility as an excuse to turn away from spiritual inquiry, just because it may rock your boat—nor as a reason to walk out on your job straightaway! Instead, slow down and breathe. Take no action. Simply be silent inside and wait … rest in being. Be totally present and simply open to the naked truth as it appears within you. Give yourself permission to feel what has been covered over by a lifetime of *shoulds* and *shouldn'ts*, to touch the vulnerability of not-knowing, to simply be still. The invitation is for you to rest in the simplicity of being and then to move from here.

Moving from the stillness and silence of being gives you the freedom to start wherever you are, without having to change, fix, or improve anything. Whatever your job description, responsibilities, daily tasks, and whatever your thoughts and feelings about it, simply be *here*, fully present. When work stops being a means to an end, it becomes the doorway to transformation. When you are willing to stop looking for security, status, fortune, or fame from what you do, and instead you are simply but utterly present in what you do, work becomes spiritual practice. It's not about bringing your spiritual qualities to work; you don't have to be calm, loving, or even compassionate when boundaries are violated, you're treated unfairly, or you're bullied or ignored. It's also not about having a job that fits in with your spiritual ideologies. It's really not about the external form, which is likely to change over time. It's about your inner state of consciousness. What you do does not matter, but *how* you do it does.

Work invites you to be exactly where you are; to be fully present with all energetic waves as they appear in you. When you feel frustration, irritation, resentment, tension, or any other difficult feeling, don't recoil or retaliate, stay in tender openness. Your willingness to simply be open offers the possibility of knowing the space within you, in which everything comes and goes. This doesn't necessarily happen all at once, but if you are willing to be softly rooted in your belly rather than jumping into your head with the rights and wrongs of the situation, the power of acceptance is likely to transform even the most mundane, or seemingly unspiritual, of jobs. Acceptance is not something you do; it *is* you ... as openness. In this openness, your feelings, your boss, your colleagues, your job, and *you* all return to spaciousness. You may or may not speak or act from this spaciousness, but if you do it will have a very different quality (and most likely a very different outcome) than speaking or acting from the noisiness of ego's defensive or manipulative strategies.

The first possible outcome is that you find peace within your daily work. Whatever you are doing, whether you're sitting at a desk, standing at a till, driving a car, climbing a ladder, negotiating a business deal, or making a cup of tea, you sense the aliveness of this moment *as it is*. If you are very silent (non-reactive) within this sense of aliveness, you'll likely also experience a subtle stream of energy just below the surface of your conscious awareness. If you stay present within this stream of energy, you may find that it brings a lightness to what you do. You may also start to enjoy what you do. Enjoyment has nothing to do with the content of what you do and everything to do with the space within which this content is takes place. If you simply enjoy without grasping on to the enjoyment, the light of beingness flows into what you do. This is when transformation happens from within, and it's likely that external situations will also transform to match your internal state of consciousness.

The second possible outcome is that it becomes very clear to you that you've been pretending to be someone you're not, and now this pretense is untenable. As you sit inside this feeling (without recoiling or reacting) something moves in you, and you either find the courage to leave your job or you wait until an opportunity appears that matches your inner state of consciousness. It's likely, as you wait and stay open, that an invitation that speaks to your authentic voice arrives seemingly "out of the blue." Perhaps someone you meet unexpectedly makes you an offer, or you get promoted. Whatever happens, it opens the door to new possibilities that were not available from the perspective of struggle or conflict. It's not about manifesting a better job, a better boss, or a better salary. It's about listening to life's intelligence as it expresses itself through all appearances in your life, however seemingly wonderful or terrible.

If you devote yourself to the deeper impulse of intelligence as it moves through you, what you do will no longer be just about making a living. It will be about fully living. Whether you find peace in the work you already do, you take a leap into a new direction, or even if you leave your job and just wait in not-knowing, you are likely to be supported by a wealth of inner and outer resources you didn't previously know were available. Even though you may have to make some personal sacrifices in the early stages, you may stumble and fall, or you may be stretched beyond your comfort zone, you will be fueled by a power that is not of this world but of something much more magnificent. You could call this *enthusiasm* or *inspiration*. It's the same as saying *vital aliveness* or the *holy breath*. It's at this point that personal and divine will become one and the same, and you become an instrument of God.

CAN MONEY AND SPIRITUALITY BE FRIENDS?

Many people, especially spiritual seekers, are confused about money. Does it make us less worthy or more worthy, less spiritual or more spiritual, less free or more free? There are many conflicting beliefs, some in support of material wealth as a sign of spiritual development, good karma, or God's benevolence, and others in opposition to it as a sign of corruption. Mostly there's a belief that money and spirituality do not go together. Perhaps even now you are wondering if the conversation around money has any place in spiritual inquiry. Money is a particularly tricky subject of inquiry because there are so many layers of personal, social, cultural, and religious conditioning that contaminate our relationship with it.

It is often said that money is the root of all evil. As we look throughout history, we see many heinous actions made in the name of financial profit. Today we are witness to a huge divide between the rich and the poor that creates suffering in all sorts of ways. It seems that having money gives us power ... and power seems to corrupt. Even some spiritual and religious teachers throughout the ages (and today) have succumbed to the power of money, using it to uphold an image of self-importance and to wield authority over the masses.

It is probably for this reason that the renunciation of material accumulation is central to many traditional spiritual paths. A person without money or possessions is unable to wield much power (or harm) in the world. And they are likely to be more humble and grateful, as they are reliant on others to support them. While there may be some truth in this view, the equation of material poverty with spiritual purity is a deeply unconscious (and mistaken) belief that perpetuates inner division. If you are sincere in your desire to awaken out of the dream of separation, and you genuinely wish to embody this awakening as a living reality, you must be willing to shine the light of awareness on all inner division, even in the most unspiritual places.

The brief conversation about money offered here isn't about others' opinions, theories, or values about money. This is about getting your hands dirty in the muck of your own beliefs about money. It's about digging deep to uncover every opinion and judgment, voice of righteousness and resentment, and every whisper of envy or disgust. Do you have strong feelings against those who have vast wealth while you struggle to make ends meet? Is there a nagging discomfort because you live in relative luxury while millions starve every day? Do you believe that spiritual teachers are wrong or bad if they receive financial compensation for the dissemination of their teachings? Usually, several conflicting stories are entwined around one another to create a knot of unresolved tension around this subject. Untangling these stories by being willing to sit inside the powerful emotions that fuel them is an honest part of spiritual inquiry.

Most often these emotions are buried quite deep and require a gentle but persistent excavation before revealing themselves, and there are likely to be several energetic layers that may not always be pleasant. You may find that rage, jealousy, guilt, and shame have been lurking in the shadows, and these are often difficult to acknowledge. But if you're willing to tenderly meet these energies in the unconditioned space of an open heart, even though it feels scary, there's an even deeper inquiry that reveals itself. This has the potential to expose the root of the knot and free you from the burden of inner conflict.

If you are willing to go all the way to the root, what is revealed is something much truer than any of your beliefs about money: the basic fear of survival. Almost everyone, despite how much money they have, has a fear of lack of money. For wealthy people, this fear is substantially cushioned, and it may never rise to conscious awareness. But the vast majority of people (including those who are quite wealthy) carry a deep-seated fear of not having enough money. For several thousands of years, the world has functioned by bartering goods and exchanging money for services. Food, shelter, clothing, and other basic living necessities have all been dependent on having some kind of currency of exchange. Without money (at least in the world we currently live in) we are homeless, hungry, and helpless, and we may even face death. Money, when stripped of opinion, judgment, and grievances, is synonymous with survival of human life.

The gift of including money in spiritual inquiry has nothing to do with replacing negative or self-limiting beliefs about money with more positive ones. The gift is to reveal the raw reality of death when the fear of lack of money is faced, and to point you to a deeper dimension of being that cannot die and is inherently wealthy. This wealth doesn't tie you to the world; it frees you, because your self-identity is no longer wrapped up with how much money you have, but instead is rooted in the abundance of your true nature.

Every time you make a financial transaction and every time you think about money, you are offered this possibility of freedom. Whether you're experiencing financial ruin, homelessness, or just the thought of not having enough, by facing this consciously (being fully present in it), the primal fear of survival can be seen for what it is: a simple fact of our earthly reality. If you are willing to deeply accept this fact without the overlay of "poor me," there is a liberation of energy that allows money to function in its rightful role as a support for life on earth. Without the attempt to grasp or hoard, and without the contamination of your beliefs, money is free to circulate where it is needed, and you are free to take care of what needs to be taken care of to support your life in an earthly body.

THE TRUE MEANING OF ABUNDANCE

Abundance is everywhere. It's in the innumerable shades of green when the breeze blows through the grass. It's in the thousands of crisp golden leaves underfoot in the fall. It's in the millions of stars clustered in the night sky. It's in the unrelenting rain of a stormy day, in the gushing of a river on its way to the sea, in the frolicking of a newborn foal in spring, and in the exuberance of morning birdsong. Abundance is the natural state of everything that is alive.

You, too, by nature, are abundant, which is why you want to *feel* abundant. Everybody wants to feel it. The storekeeper wants to feel the security of the profit in his till at the end of the day. The businessman wants to feel the satisfaction of successful projects. The fisherman wants to feel good about the size of his catch as he returns home to shore. The hungry child wants to feel the fullness of her belly. Even an alcoholic wants to feel the warmth of alcohol coursing through his veins. While this may seem in opposition to the idea of abundance, it is the same desire to feel abundant that is driving this action. Feeling abundant gives us a sense of contentment, groundedness, safety, and goodness—a sense of fullness or completeness.

While abundance itself is natural, the *wanting* to feel abundant is not, unless it has to do with the natural impulse of basic survival needs, such as hunger. Wanting means lack. It means you are asking life to give you something to make you feel complete. Unless the core belief in lack is exposed as a false construct, no matter how much you accumulate it will be empty of true abundance. The attempt to *have* something in order to feel abundant is a byproduct of the unilluminated mind. It's not really about the amount of your bank balance, the size of your house, or the number of trophies you have. It's about feeling worthy. For the majority of humanity, which functions in an egoic state of consciousness, having more (especially more money) is a sign of one's worth. While this is true on a literal level, it is absolute nonsense from a psychological or spiritual perspective.

A surprising number of people, especially in today's materially oriented world, experience a lack of self-worth. There's a common belief, even in spiritual circles, that not having enough money is a sign of unworthiness. This usually translates into "I am unable to receive," "I don't love myself," or "I'm not good enough." What often follows is an attempt to improve self-worth in order to attract more money in order to *feel* abundant, and therefore to believe yourself to be worthy. Sometimes this works (at least for a while), but mostly it does not. The acquisition of psychological and spiritual tools for fixing yourself and getting what you want in order to feel better about yourself is a huge error of attention. By giving allegiance to the story of "me" and "my life," the ping-pong of feeling worthy and feeling unworthy is prolonged. It's a perpetuation of the seeking mechanism, and there is no fulfillment in this.

If this ping-pong game is familiar to you (and you are truly tired of it), I invite you to take a pause here. Take a moment to turn within and ask yourself, "What happens when I don't have what I want, when I don't get the recognition, approval, or profit? What would happen if I lost everything? Who am I when my bank balance is zero, my home's been taken away, or my creative project is a flop? What would I be worth? And who is it that decides my worth?"

Do not attempt to answer these questions from your mind. Simply be present, listen, and *feel* the answer in your heart and in your belly. Be totally honest with yourself. Do you feel worthless? Do you feel that your life has no value, that you're a failure, or that you're a waste of space? Allow yourself to get right up close and intimate with the feelings that reveal themselves. Don't turn away or hide in shame. Simply breathe, and be *here*. Allow yourself to taste the flavor of worthlessness, to touch the texture of failure, to sit inside the sensation of being a waste of space. And now ask yourself if any of this is really true, now, in *this* moment? Can you really find worthlessness … *here*? Can you really find failure … *here*? Can your life really be a waste of time when your life is what is here as the reality of *now*? And can you find anyone who is the one who decides your worth? Do they actually exist *now*, in *this* moment? Don't jump back into your head; simply breathe and be here. Keep inviting the question to land in your belly.

Perhaps, as you lose yourself in the unboundedness of this moment, you will realize (not in your mind as a thought, but as a visceral sense in your deepest knowing) that your life cannot possibly be a waste of time, but where you give your attention can be. Maybe you will realize that you cannot possibly be a failure, but that you have simply failed to see what is already here. Or you may see, once and for all, that abundance doesn't come from what you *have*; it is what you *are*.

When you fulfill your inner purpose of awakening to your true nature as the unboundedness of being, the polarity of worthiness and unworthiness collapses into the totality of *now*. You do not need to *feel* abundant, because abundance is *here* as the fullness of this moment. There is no one to judge you as worthy or unworthy. It was only ever yourself judging yourself. When you awaken out of the dream of separation, this is seen to be ludicrous (and a waste of time)! When you stop right *here* and rest deeply in the softness of your belly, in the gentle throb of your heartbeat, in the pregnant pause between each breath, in the alive awakeness of now, you may well discover that this moment is rich beyond measure, and that there is no limit to abundance.

In discovering your true nature *as* abundance, it does not matter what material things you have or don't have or whether you have everything you want or none of it at all. All of it, even the apparent lack, is experienced as the fullness of life's offering. It's not about the content because all content comes and goes. It's about the depth of your presence and the breadth of your openness. You come to know this when you stop waiting for the world to fill up the hole inside, and live life fully … *now*.

LIVE FULL, DIE EMPTY

As you come to the final pages of this book, you may be excited by the very real possibility of living a fully awake life, here and now. Perhaps some of your questions about how the truth of this awakening can be lived in the midst of everyday life have been answered. And new questions are arising within you in this very moment. It is, of course, an ongoing conversation, and an inquiry that continues in the intimacy of your own heart as you encounter and embrace the messiness of being human. The real question is: Are you willing, whether your experience is tranquil, turbulent, ecstatic, tragic, opulent, or austere, to give yourself wholeheartedly to what is truly alive in you?

Are you willing to stop waiting for the right time (when you're rich enough, safe enough, strong enough, or enlightened enough), and give every ounce of yourself to *this* precious (and fleeting) moment? To be so intimate with this earthly experience that you find the sacred in the mundane and the beauty in the horror and the glory in the brokenness? Are you willing to inhale so deeply that not a vestige of resistance remains in you and every last drop of your life is fully taken in? Are you willing to let it all go on an exhale? Because that's what it takes to end the suffering of an unilluminated mind and to live as the light of consciousness.

Whether you live a life of fortune, fame, or failure, the invitation is for you to live fully and to die empty: to be fully here as "you" in the movie called "your life." To *feel* fully, to *love* fully, to enjoy the riches and the acclaim, to enjoy the comforts and the pleasures, to enjoy the fullness of earthly life, but to not wrap your story of "special me" around it or embellish it with meaning. With every breath (whether it's the breath in *this* moment or the very last breath of your life) you can let "your life" go. You can relinquish the addiction to past-fear and future-hope so that you may enter this moment naked and unencumbered. This is what is meant by the words of Jesus: "It is easier for a camel to pass through the eye of a needle, than for a rich man to enter the kingdom of heaven."[8] The "rich man" in this saying is not necessarily someone with a lot of money, property, or possessions, but someone who invests a lot of meaning in his or her wealth (material wealth, the accumulation of skills, or spiritual knowledge) and constructs a mountain of beliefs about being worthy or special. If you truly want to enter the "kingdom of heaven" and be free of suffering, you must put down the burden of all acquisitions and be fully here, in *this* moment, without a story. This freedom is available to you here and *now* if you are willing to die, in *this* moment, as empty awakeness.

A Final Invitation

What does it mean to live a fully human yet fully awakened life? It means the willingness to stop your journey of seeking, right here, in *this* moment. Whether or not your journey of seeking has been a golden thread of promise that you've clung to through this lifetime or an accumulation of lifetimes, it has brought you to *this* moment right *here*, right *now*. In the eternal unfoldment of this moment, if you are willing (without a doubt) to stop following the seeking mechanism of the egoic mind and turn your attention back to your innermost being, the *yes* of your inherently awake consciousness can meet the *yes* that drives the evolutionary momentum of existence.

That which is already awake in you (awakeness itself) seeks you as much as you seek awakeness. The impulse of consciousness to know itself as the totality of you is as great as the impulse of your innermost desire to seek the freedom of unbounded consciousness. Both of these impulses are evolutionary processes: one is the outward movement from formlessness to form, the other is the inward movement from form to formlessness. Together, they are the expression of consciousness attempting to become awake to itself.

At the absolute level, consciousness is already awake. It is fully alive in its pristine awakeness *as* formlessness. But as it descends into the relative level (and as the words in this book have pointed to, over and over again), it easily gets lost in the identification with form. You, with your capacity for self-reflection, are the portal through which consciousness can become aware of itself. You, with your capacity to choose where attention goes, are responsible for consciousness returning to itself. When the dream of separation becomes unbearable, and you have the courage to honestly say you have had enough of suffering, then awareness has the possibility to turn back in on itself and recognize the deeper dimension of formlessness that exists prior to all forms.

When you become fully aware of that which is inherently awake in you, not only are you liberated from identification with form, but so is consciousness. In this way, consciousness evolves through you *as* you. This is why your *yes* plays such a crucial role in the future of all life. You as the "I" you think you are doesn't matter one iota. But *you* as the awakeness revealed *through* form absolutely matters! If you are finally willing to say an unequivocal *yes* to this invitation to awaken, a new consciousness and a new humanity is born in this very moment—even now, as you read these words.

Acknowledgments

A number of angels have assisted me in birthing this book into the world. I am deeply grateful to Shanti Einolander for her priceless feedback and loving encouragement. To Julian Noyce for opening the door to a new possibility. And to Catharine Meyers at New Harbinger Publications for the immensity of her vision, passion, and support. I also would like to thank the incredible team at New Harbinger for all their input, especially Heather Garnos and Erin Raber for their editorial skills. A big thank you to John Welwood for providing a heartfelt foreword to this book.

I am also grateful to those who offered a safe haven for writing when life's vicissitudes threatened to interrupt the creative process: Martina Stahl in Stockholm, Roxana Noor in Kings Langley, and Kerry Maisey in Hastings. And to Kavi, my husband and beloved, for giving me the space when I needed it and for holding my hand at other times; your devotion and support are a blessing to me. Last but not least, I am grateful to my mother, who passed away halfway through my journey of writing this book, but whose presence I have felt every step of the way.

Notes

CHAPTER 3

1. Schucman, H. and Thetford, W. 1975. *A Course in Miracles.* Mill Valley, CA: Foundation for Inner Peace.

CHAPTER 4

2. John 2:17 (New American Standard Bible)

CHAPTER 5

3. Lomax, E. 1995. *The Railway Man.* New York, NY: Vintage.

4. Luke 23:34 (New American Standard Bible)

CHAPTER 6

5. Gospel of Thomas 113

6. Dass, Ram. 2001. *Still Here.* New York, NY: Riverhead Books.

CHAPTER 9

7. Szekely, E.B. 1981. *The Essene Gospel of Peace.* Paris: International Biogenic Society.

CHAPTER 10

8. Mark 10:25 (New American Standard Bible)

Amoda Maa is a contemporary spiritual teacher, author, and speaker. After years of spiritual seeking, meditation, and immersion in psychospiritual practices, an experience of the dark night of the soul led her to a profound inner awakening. Then, after a long period of integration, she began speaking from silence in small gatherings. She offers meetings and retreats, and is a frequent speaker at conferences and events, attracting spiritual seekers and people looking for peace and fulfillment in an increasingly chaotic world. Her teachings are free of religion and tradition, and she brings to them a deep understanding of the human journey, born out of her own experience.

Amoda Maa is author of *Radical Awakening* (formerly *How to Find God in Everything*) and *Change Your Life, Change Your World*, both of which arose out of a mystical vision around the time of her awakening. In this vision, she was shown the key to humanity's suffering and the potential for the birth of a new consciousness and world. *Embodied Enlightenment* is based on both her vision for humanity and the conversations on the cutting edge of spiritual inquiry in her meetings with people from all around the world. She lives with her husband and beloved, Kavi, in California. To learn more, visit http://www.amodamaa.com.

Foreword writer **John Welwood, PhD**, is a psychotherapist, author, and teacher specializing in the integration of Eastern spiritual wisdom and Western psychology. His books include *Journey of the Heart*, *Perfect Love, Imperfect Relationships*, and *Toward a Psychology of Awakening*.

MORE BOOKS for the SPIRITUAL SEEKER

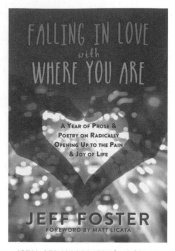

ISBN: 978-1908664396 | US $16.95

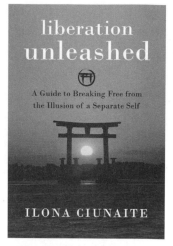

ISBN: 978-1626258068 | US $16.95

ISBN: 978-1626258808 | US $19.95

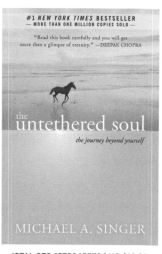

ISBN: 978-1572245372 | US $16.95

🌱 new**harbinger**publications

✿ NON-DUALITY PRESS | ◐ SAHAJA | ✾ REVEAL PRESS